EAST RENFREWSHIRE COUNCIL

0825185 1

iip **Glenister** is known to millions as DCI Gene Hunt
the BBC's hit series *Life on Mars* and *Ashes to Ashes*. An
ard-winning actor, he has also starred in *Cranford*,
ilendar Girls, *State of Play* and *Clocking Off*, among many
her shows. He lives in London with his wife and two
ughters.

THINGS AIN'T WHAT THEY USED TO BE

Philip Glenister

Edited by Philip Dodd

Sphere
An imprint of
Little, Brown Book Group
100 Victoria Embankment
London EC4Y 0DY

An Hachette UK Company
www.hachette.co.uk

www.littlebrown.co.uk

SPHERE

First published in Great Britain in 2008 by Sphere
This paperback edition published in 2009 by Sphere

Copyright © Philip Glenister 2008

The moral right of the author has been asserted.

All rights reserved.
No part of this publication may be reproduced, stored in a
retrieval system, or transmitted, in any form or by any means, without
the prior permission in writing of the publisher, nor be otherwise circulated
in any form of binding or cover other than that in which it is published
and without a similar condition including this condition
being imposed on the subsequent purchaser.

A CIP catalogue record for this book
is available from the British Library.

ISBN 978-0-7515-4206-6

Typeset in Palatino by M Rules
Printed and bound in Great Britain by
Clays Ltd, St Ives plc

Papers used by Sphere are natural, renewable and
recyclable products sourced from well-managed forests and certified
in accordance with the rules of the Forest Stewardship Council.

Mixed Sources
Product group from well-managed
forests and other controlled sources
www.fsc.org Cert no. SGS-COC-004081
© 1996 Forest Stewardship Council
FSC

EAST RENFREWSHIRE COUNCIL	
0825185 1	
HJ	21-May-2009
941.085	£6.99
	NE

For Beth, Millie and Charlotte, without whom . . .

. . . I'd be loaded

Introduction

One of the best things about nostalgia is sharing it with others. This book was prompted by some of the memories people have shared with me over the years and particularly since I first ponced on to the screen as DCI Gene Hunt. But what's interesting is that it's not just the thirty, forty and fifty-somethings who come up and say how much they've enjoyed reminiscing about their childhood and teens, thanks to *Life on Mars* and *Ashes to Ashes*. It's also the current crop of teenagers, who say they now understand a little better what their parents keep banging on about.

I've enjoyed putting this book together, and I hope it triggers some treasured memories of your own. If it also throws up some long-buried images of yourself in high-waisted flares, smooching to 'Every Day Hurts' by Sad Café at the local youth club, don't blame me. This book is not for the faint-hearted.

So, with that in mind, let's tear open the wrapper of nostalgia and sink our teeth into the Walnut Whip of reminiscence . . .

Curly Wurly or Green & Black's

Chocolate bars

31 May 1970 The ninth World Cup kicks off at the Estadio Azteca in Mexico City – this, along with the Olympics two years earlier, promotes a wave of interest in all things Mexican, which is celebrated by Cadbury's launch of the late, lamented Aztec bar.

I've lost count of the number of times I've been asked about the Curly Wurly bar, and whether they used to be larger. It's one of the great unanswered questions of the 1970s and '80s, right up there with whatever really happened to Lord Lucan, and whoever thought it was a good idea to perm Kevin Keegan's hair?

Now, I thought, I was going to set the record straight, once and for all, bang to rights. On *Life on Mars*, there's a scene where I stir my cup of tea with a Curly Wurly, and since attention to period detail was paramount, the props guys acquired an original Curly Wurly wrapper from a collector. (A sideline here. What kid in their right mind collected, cleaned and preserved sweet wrappers on the off-chance that in later life they could provide them as props for retro TV shows? The same goes for those mint-condition Corgi James Bond Aston Martins you can find on eBay, or the Action Man in full paratrooper outfit but still in his box, *unopened*! If you got one for Christmas the packaging would have been ripped off in nanoseconds. I never met a kid who'd pause, reflect and say, 'Thank you, Mater, but I will set this toy to one side, if you don't mind. And later, while the rest of you are chuckling at *The Morecambe and Wise Christmas Special*, I shall be working out the cost–benefit analysis for my museum of nostalgia.' Oh yeah. Well, piss off, son.) Anyway, this genuine 1970s Curly Wurly wrapper pitched up on set. A runner was dispatched to buy some new Curly Wurlies and we managed to fit at least two, if not three, of the modern-day bars inside that wrapper. Proof conclusive, or so I thought. But then I heard that Cadbury's official line is that they've never changed the size of them – so for the time being we'll have to fudge the issue (that's a finger of fudge, of course).

So join me in a stroll to the shelves of my virtual tuck shop. My school didn't believe in tuck shops, but Susanne's Riding Stables nearby did, and every Saturday morning my best mate Paul Paterson and I would hike across fields to spend some pocket money. Once we arrived, one fun little pastime was to buy a Supermousse bar or two – now long gone – and surreptitiously feed it to the horses, who would start frothing at the mouth before charging off in the grip of a massive equine sugar rush.

Let's chew over the chocolate bars of yesteryear, the Wagon Wheels, Double Deckers and Topic bars (old joke: What has a hazelnut in every bite? Squirrel shit). The Curly Wurly's a given, though Terry Scott dressed as a Krankie in the ads was a bit disconcerting. The Cadbury's Creme Egg, which was only available in the run-up to

Easter, as it should be. The Texan, as tough as John Wayne's leathery hide and guaranteed to take your teeth out. The Walnut Whip – you didn't do the walnut, just ignored it completely, and went straight for the cream (just like the Sherbet Dab, where the liquorice stick was jettisoned and the sherbet downed like a yard of ale). The sugary snap, crackle and pop of Moon Dust – what was that all about? No other food stuff known to man behaves like that. And that other 'food of the future', Flying Saucers – basically two bits of pastel-coloured paper with some unidentified powdered fizz in the middle.

On the way home from school we would drop in on an old lady close by, who kept a cupboard bursting with sweets for sale – pink shells, sweet cigarettes, Bazooka Joe . . . the works. There would be a line of kids queuing all the way down her hall and out on to the street, forming an orderly conveyor belt, jiggling the coins in their pockets and trying to work out if they had enough for a quarter-pound of Cola Cubes. Somehow I can't imagine that happening today. A little old lady selling teeth-rotting sweeties to the local kids? They'd slap an ASBO on her faster than you could say 'ten Black Jacks, please'.

It's amazing that we were being sold the idea that chocolate was actually a kind of health food: that old Dairy Milk sales line about their being 'a glass and a half of milk in every bar', as if our teeth and bones would all crumble to dust if we didn't take heed. Or that a finger of fudge was 'full of Cadbury goodness', or the suggestion that a 'Mars a day helps you work, rest and play' – like it was an apple. Maybe they should add a Terry's Chocolate

Orange to those lists of five fruit and veg we're supposed to eat a day.

Like everyone else, I can savour the refinement and the exquisite taste of the cocoa heaven offered by a bar of Green & Black's 85% Dark, and appreciate the sustainability of the whole enterprise. But I still hark back to the legendary After Eight mint. Extracting each square from its little paper sleeve was like opening a tiny present – right until the point when you found some other greedy bugger – usually your nan – had left you with a boxful of empty wrappers!

Mousetrap or Wii

Fun for all the family

25 December 1970 New Waddington's board games for this Christmas include Air Charter, based on air cargo trading in the Pacific, Cube Fusion, a modular strategy game, Discovery and the Great Downhill Ski Game.

End of term. The final day before summer beckoned, six weeks of freedom, and the class has been allowed to bring in a game from home. 'Hey, sir, why not let us have the day off instead?' was my attitude, but at least there was a phenomenal number of games to choose from: Operation, Buckaroo, Othello, Connect Four, Monopoly, Cluedo, Sorry!, and the less common Waddington games like Thunderbirds and Blast-Off! If some oaf had Escape from Colditz, though, you didn't get involved: it was so bloody complicated that you'd have been banged up in the classroom until the start of the next term. Another kid would always bring in Mousetrap and have one vital piece missing. Close your eyes and you can imagine that crazy sequence: crank, gears, lever, boot, bucket, ball, stairs, pipe, rod with hands, bowling ball, groove, bathtub, diver, bucket and cage!

Remember a board game called Buccaneer? It was full of tiny diamonds, pearls and rubies as well as miniature barrels of rum. Spirograph was addictive, although in the end what was the point of creating those patterns? Beats me. Oh, and Striker (a simpler version of Subbuteo), featuring a pitch with little goals, players who kicked when you pressed their heads down, and diving goalkeepers.

Simple things, hours of good, clean fun – mangling limbs on the Twister mat, teasing out the straws from the KerPlunk tube. It really was, as the strapline said, 'for all the family'. Are there any games for all the (dysfunctional) family these days? Since most kids are holed up in their rooms locked on to their games console, I doubt it. Maybe the Wii's the closest. But just like sitting round the dining-room table for Sunday lunch, playing games together may have gone for ever. Time for a little thinking *inside* the box.

Lashings of gravy or a drizzle of jus

Food, glorious food

23 January 1971 Prog rock is the order of the day as Gravy Train, a Lancashire-based band led by Norman Barratt and J. D. Hughes, release their eponymous debut album on the Vertigo label.

The 1970s was a decade when us Brits finally tried – not always successfully – to expand the frontiers of our culinary knowledge. We didn't get that far to be honest – just about to the foothills of the Swiss Alps before retreating with a plundered fondue set – but we tried.

From the vantage point of the snooty interior of a bespoke kitchen gleaming with Gaggenau, or the cool interior of a Nigella-inspired pantry crammed with herbs, spices and pulses from every known continent, those first fumbling steps towards a little taste-bud adventure look so kitsch. But my stomach and I have a real fondness for those years, when a Vesta pack of Chicken Supreme with its little foil packets seemed as unimaginably exotic as the food they were serving on board *Apollo 14*.

Yes, this was an age before sushi – raw fish, that's just *wrong* – when sophistication at any party was all about producing a hedgehog of pineapple and cheese cubes, and the humble vol-au-vent was positively rakish. An age

when your mum's early attempt at a lasagne would pro-
voke mutters from a grizzly great-uncle of 'I'm not eating
that foreign muck, love', but she'd persevere with the coq
au vin the family had first tasted on a camping trip to
France. To this day, my mum calls the family to dinner in
French. '*À table*', she cries.

This was also the age of the gadget. Soda siphons that
splurged and spurted great geysers of fizzy nothing into a
slug of Campari. The Hostess trolley wheeled silently,
almost menacingly, across the wall-to-wall carpet. And the
electric carving knife, truly cutting-edge technology. My
old man still has the one he bought in the '70s, preserved
in its original packaging, always on hand just in case we
need to call him in for some precision carving or an emergency Caesarean.

We also used the magnificent egg slicer that could gar-
rotte a hard-boiled egg in the twinkling of an eye, ready
for each slice to be slathered in Heinz salad cream. And
there was the mincer, screwed on to the kitchen table with
a cranking handle straight off a Model T Ford, perfect for
recycling the Sunday roast for the rest of the week, until
Friday and fish came around. There was something
hugely reassuring about knowing what you were going to
be eating each day of the week, even if the two veg were
sweltered to within an inch of their lives – another of my
mum's *bon mots*, whenever we serve her some lightly stir-
fried carrots, is: 'Unlike you, Phil, I like my vegetables
cooked.'

We ate simple fare, unpretentiously, and maybe that's
why my blood boils (at 220° Celsius – or should that be

Regulo 7?) when I read ridiculous descriptions of good old British food in overwrought restaurant menus. 'Entrecôte of hand-reared Kobe beef, tenderly grilled, on a bed of Bedford Browns with a nest of pommes frites' . . . Steak, egg and chips, my son. 'Crevettes enrobed in a coating of vine-ripened tomato purée, hand-ground cayenne and home-produced sauce mayonnaise'? That's a prawn cocktail, pal.

And please don't get me started on jus. Jus? *Jus?* If it's gravy, call it gravy. Gravy should be back-strengthening stuff, solid enough to stand a spoon to attention in it. Now, I know my way round a few swanky restaurants. I've even been to Nobu. But wherever I might be I refuse the jus. The jus will never pass my lips. Not ever. And, by the way, this is not just any old rant. This is an M&S rant.

Chopper Harris or JT

Football's hard men

21 May 1971 Ron 'Chopper' Harris, captain of Chelsea, lifts the Cup Winner's Cup, the club's first major European honour, after they beat Real Madrid 2–1 in a replay in Athens, Peter Osgood scoring the winning goal.

Whatever happened to proper football nicknames? Those nicknames for all the really hard men in the game. I'm talking about the kind of defenders who would spit at the whole idea that getting a nudge on the ball was more important than taking a large, preferably bloody, chunk of raw flesh out of an opponent first. Especially if the opponent in question was an over-talented, twinkle-toed cocky little bugger like Bestie or Rodney Marsh or Johan Cruyff whose searing (it was always *searing*) pace would leave you stone-cold dead or who could make you look a numpty by nutmegging you with millions watching on TV, all sniggering at your leaden-footed incompetence.

You know what I mean. The kind of nickname sported by Leeds United's finest, Norman 'Bites Yer Legs' Hunter, a man never knowingly ready to pull out of a tackle. And yes, I know he had a cultured left foot and was Player of the Year and all that, but he was hard, hard, hard. Les Cocker, the Leeds trainer, was once told that

Norman had gone home with a broken leg. 'Whose is it?' he asked.

Same era: Norman's team-mate Johnny 'Harmer' Giles, great nickname. Or Tommy Smith, the 'Anfield Iron'. Bill Shankly had a great phrase about him – 'Tommy Smith wasn't born, he was quarried.' And Chelsea's Ron 'Chopper' Harris.

Forget the beautiful game, this was pure ugly.

They're an extinct breed these days. Some of the last-known specimens were 'Razor' Ruddock and Vinnie Jones, a.k.a. the 'Axe'. Vinnie was on the pitch not for his silky skills, but to put a vice-like grip on Gazza's wedding tackle. Here's a line from the eminently quotable Tommy Docherty. 'Vinnie,' he said, 'could trap a ball further than I could kick it.' Which reminds me of a similar comment Ian Baker-Finch made about golfer John Daly: 'His driving is unbelievable. I don't go that far on my holidays.'

Now what have we got? Chopper's twenty-first-century equivalent, John Terry, Stamford Bridge's resident hard man, or at least as hard as he's allowed to be in the non-contact era, even if he did start blubbing after messing up in the small matter of the Champions League shoot-out. His nickname is 'JT'. Come on! JT is not a nickname for a hard man. It's a nickname for the guy who swans up to you at TGI Friday's and tells you he's going to be your server for the night, then asks which speciality cocktail you would like.

Becks and Lamps, no thank you. These are nicknames suitable only for men who shave their chest hair. Can you imagine Billy Bremner lathering up with Veet? No!

When I first started watching football it was the Chopper era, defenders and bikes. Wealdstone FC was my local club, once of the Isthmian League, and champions of the Southern League First Division (South) in 1973/4 thanks almost entirely to our star striker, George Duck. Cold, foggy, smoggy Saturday afternoons. Dodgy floodlights. Standing in those baggy trousers with pockets in line with your knees, blue and white scarf, even wearing rosettes. Unbelievable. We'd all cram in behind one goal. The away fans all stuck behind their goal. And huge aching voids on the terraces in between. A cup of Bovril ... and Bovril crisps, just in case we hadn't had enough of a beefy fix.

Players with shinguards that wouldn't have been out of place on Russell Crowe in *Gladiator*. And boots that a miner would have felt safe in, huge studs, leather as thick as your arm, doused in dubbin (whatever happened to dubbin?), not the ballet pumps they ponce about in these days. Nobody ever cracked their metatarsals. Or at least they never complained about it if they did. We didn't even know what a metatarsal was – a dinosaur, maybe?

The great thing was that you could see wonderful players. Back then the professionals kept on going long after their glory days. Jimmy Greaves turned out for Brentford and then Barnet. And at a pro-celebrity match you'd get Bobby Moore – *Bobby Moore* – turning up at Wealdstone for a kickabout. Then, when their legs finally gave up, they'd go and open a pub – Tommy Smith ran one called the Anfield Iron, naturally.

Oh, and we had our own hard men at Wealdstone.

Some chap who was to become internationally renowned as Psycho – known as Mr Stuart Pearce to you and me – joined in 1978, and Vinnie Jones played for the club in the mid-'80s. Now I'm not saying I miss those days of hard men and harder knocks, but at least there were no pampered strikers rolling around in supposed agony just because the centre back looked at them funny. There'll be a category created for them by BAFTA soon. You mark my words.

Fenn Street or Hogwarts

Fictional schools

14 June 1971 Second reading of the bill proposed by then Education Secretary Margaret Thatcher to end the delivery of free milk to schoolkids aged seven or more, hence her nickname: 'Thatcher, Thatcher, Milk Snatcher'.

I was desperately trying to remember the name of the kid in *Please, Sir!*, that seminal school sitcom from the late '60s and early '70s, who thought he was tough, with his black leather jacket, but who was actually a real mummy's boy. ('How's my little soldier?' she'd ask as she picked him up at the gate. 'Oh, Mum,' he'd reply.) I couldn't get it at all. Then it came to me: Frankie Abbott. Of course. And all the other names of the Fenn Street kids flowed naturally, like hearing the register of class 5C read out. Wisecracking Duffy ('Oy, chief!'), dishy Sharon, timid, intense Maureen, lovable but dense Dennis (all the girls loved to mother him) and smooth Peter Craven. They all looked like they were well into their twenties, indeed probably were, and certainly a lot older than John Alderton as 'Privet' Hedges, the object of Maureen's secret crush, who gallantly attempted to maintain some semblance of order – 'Now I'm sure Duffy meant no ethnic malice, Wesley.'

The teaching staff were a sitcom in their own right. The

indomitable Doris Ewell was played by Joan Sanderson, later the most infuriating of all the guests to take a room at Fawlty Towers. She was a prototype Margaret Thatcher to Mr Price's Neil Kinnock (and the indecisive headmaster's David Steel), trying to deal with a new world, while the old, soon-to-be-discarded world was represented by Deryck Guyler's uniformed caretaker Potter and Erik Chitty's antediluvian Mr Smith.

I had the chance to work with John Alderton on *Calendar Girls* – he'd also worked with my father a few years back – and it was one of those strange, rather nice moments that happen in acting now and again, when somebody I'd watched and admired as a kid was now sitting across the other side of the table in a Yorkshire pub.

If the antics at Fenn Street were simply fun to watch, *Grange Hill* was much closer to the schooldays I knew. I went to secondary school in 1975 – the first intake as our local area went comprehensive, part of the great '70s education revolution. My brother Robert had taken the 11+, but everything changed as I came to the end of primary school. In fact we were held back a year while they rejigged everything, like some kind of junior Guantanamo Bay, and then released as the new system's guinea pigs into what had previously been Blackwell Secondary Modern, now rebranded Hatch End High to remove the stigma of streaming. The old Harrow County Grammar School – which Michael Portillo and Diane Abbott (and my old man) had attended – also had a makeover and was unveiled as Gayton.

Grange Hill started in 1978 and absolutely mirrored this

new comprehensive lifestyle. So for me watching Tucker Jenkins was like staring at a reflection – my generation could really relate to this series. Odd, then, to find that where the strength of *Grange Hill* was that very sense of authenticity and realism, the most popular fictional school of the last ten years has been the traditional, fantastical Hogwarts. And there seems to be no shortage of applicants to go on reality TV programmes that stick inner-city kids in a grammar school or a '50s-style public school to lick 'em into shape. Has anybody thought of rounding up a posse of Hooray Henrys and plonking them into the local sink school for a term to see how *they*'d get on? Now, that's what I call entertainment.

The Raymond Revuebar or Spearmint Rhino

Gentleman's clubs

June 1971 The 'King of Porn', Paul Raymond, who had opened his Revuebar in 1958, relaunches *Men Only* and swiftly establishes it as one of the essential '70s top-shelf magazines.

I worked for a while in Soho in the early '80s. There was a celebrated whorehouse just round the corner. As I took a short cut past it each morning, I would invariably be accosted by some hooker, asking me, 'Would you like a girl, darling?' 'Yes, but not you, love . . .' This was when Soho still had some of the old seedy glow, before it was spruced up. There are now only a handful of those strip clubs and peep shows left. Paul Raymond's Revuebar was up on Wardour Street. And Madame Jojo's was on Brewer Street, very much a 1980s icon. Whenever I walked past the drag queens outside with a girlfriend she'd moan that it wasn't fair that blokes could have such good legs. In fact, I did once say, 'Look at the arse on that!' and the leotarded geezer in question gave me a very fine rabbit punch in the back as a riposte as I walked past. One night inside the club, just after Fred Astaire had died, the cabaret artiste sang a tribute to him to the tune of 'I'm in Heaven' – 'Fred's in Heaven'. Well, Fred might not have been, but

Boy George, Marilyn and Mark Almond almost certainly were.

The lap- and pole-dancing and escort clubs moved out of Soho. Now the knocking shops are all out in the City and Docklands, servicing the traders and dealers – although when the credit crunch kicked in and the bonuses dwindled, the first thing to go, said one club owner, was the spending on escorts and tarts. Drive around the streets of EC1 and there are all the clubs, still maintaining that heavy-handed air of what they think is raffishness, bow-tied door staff, smoked glass and lots of silver signage. But why oh why is Spearmint Rhino called that? Presumably Juicyfruit Jumbo and Wrigley Hippo had already been taken.

'Nice to see you, to see you . . . nice' or 'What's occurring?'

Catchphrases

2 October 1971 Bruce Forsyth – and the lovely Anthea Redfern – launch *The Generation Game*, the BBC's new Saturday evening family entertainment show.

It's amazing how an old catchphrase can bring back memories in a flash. You only have to hear Brucie's trademark 'Nice to see you . . .' and you can visualise the whole show, from the cuddly toy on the juddering conveyor belt to Anthea Redfern 'giving us a twirl'.

Every light entertainment show worth its salt had a catchphrase everyone could mimic. But even some drama shows had a few favourite sayings. Take the Sweeney, for instance. Although they weren't really catchphrases in the same way, everyone knows 'You're nicked' and 'Shut it!'. Another great line from Regan was, 'We're the Sweeney, son, and we haven't had any dinner yet.' There was quite a lot of Jack Regan in Gene Hunt. I was flattered to see a Gene line made it into an internet poll of TV catchphrases – 'You're surrounded by armed bastards!' – another great line wonderfully written (and beautifully delivered, natch) that emerged organically out of the character and the situation. And in the grime on the back of white vans you can now see 'Fire up the Quattro!' in place of 'I wish my wife was this dirty'.

Funnily enough, because the Gene Hunt lines got taken up and were listed on the net, there was definitely more pressure on the writers of *Ashes to Ashes*. It's hard to plan a one-liner, so good on performers like Harry Enfield, Catherine Tate and the *Little Britain* lads, who have created catchphrase-driven shows. I'm not a scriptwriter. Though maybe if you have a vehicle where you can repeat a line often enough it will stick in the end – Andy Millman's teeth-gritting 'Are you havin' a laff?' in *Extras* is a great parody of the genre. And when they do stick they become part of the national vocabulary. My mother Joannie has recently taken to asking, 'What's occurring?' She lives in Wales and she thinks I've never heard it before. 'It's from *Gavin and Stacey*,' she'll tell me. 'Yes, I know.'

Do other nations have as many catchphrases? It seems a uniquely British passion to sit in the pub trading them the same way that in the school playground we'd swap impressions of Frank Spencer and whoever else Mike Yarwood was impersonating at the time.

So here we are, undisputed champions of the world at catchphrases (possibly only the US could challenge us, though personally I think we'd win hands down). And what do we do? We develop a show called *Catchphrase* and it's appalling, with the worst buzzer sound ever. That must have been a prerequisite of those quiz shows, the sound boffins looking for the naffest noise they could create. Perhaps it was the same team who came up with the wrong-answer 'nuh, nuh' on *Family Fortunes*. Now, was it an urban myth, or did one contestant, when asked by Les Dennis to name a dangerous race, really slam his hand down and say, 'The Arabs'? Nuh, nuh.

Jensen Interceptor or Baby Bentley

Dream cars

20 October 1971 At the Earl's Court Motor Show, the West Bromwich-based Jensen motor company launches its SP – short for Six Pack – model, its most powerful car, mixing muscle and style.

I first saw a Jensen Interceptor when I was about ten, and my best pal Paul came rushing round to our house to tell me that a friend of his dad had turned up to visit and had parked his Interceptor on the Patersons' drive. We hotfooted it over there, where his father's friend was standing, for all the world like Graham Hill, a vision in leather jacket and sheepskin collar, with his hand resting lightly on the Interceptor's roof.

If you've never seen a Jensen Interceptor, imagine a high-performance two-door saloon with a huge, curved, wraparound rear window (which doubled as a hatchback) and with a long old bonnet. A kind of stretch Aston Martin DB5. The version Paul and I looked at longingly outside his house was tan-coloured, with a black roof, and alloys.

The Jensen, along with Roger Moore's Aston Martin DBS and Tony Curtis's Ferrari Dino from *The Persuaders*, always had top place in my fantasy car charts. I always thought it was a bit unfair they gave Tony the low chassis of the Dino, given his age – a tad uncomfortable on the old coccyx. At the time my grandparents lived in Newport Pagnell (not just a motorway service area) and I remember driving past the nearby Aston factory and seeing all these fab motors on the forecourt. Nowadays, footballers and wannabes hanker after a Bentley Continental GT convertible, the 'Baby Bentley'.

My first experience of driving was in a Ford Fiesta, a local driving instructor's car. It stank of stale roll-ups – hardly the *Persuaders*-style glamour I'd been looking forward to – and I changed instructors soon after he started using the afternoon lessons to get me to drive round to his house, whereupon he'd disappear inside and emerge half an hour later while I sat in the road outside. I was clearly being used as a paying chauffeur while the guy had a quick cuppa or something more saucy.

I took my driving test as soon as I could, and, like all the best drivers, promptly failed at the first attempt, having contrived to drive over a double roundabout. Next, I heard the examiner tell me to turn left, which I obediently did, straight into a car park. 'What are you doing?' he asked. We decided there wasn't much point in going any further after that.

The birds or the bees

Talking, or not talking, about sex

12 June 1972 World premiere in New York of *Deep Throat*, starring Linda Lovelace and with the tagline: 'How far does a girl have to go to untangle her tingle?'

According to that other legendary Phil, the Larkin one, sex began in 1963, 'Between the end of the *Chatterley* ban/And the Beatles' first LP'. Great line. But if that was when sex was invented, by the time a young P. Glenister was taking his first tentative steps into that murky world, it felt like it still hadn't been released to the general public, at least not in my small corner of the world. As a teenager, I knew it was out there somewhere, but, like a Jensen Interceptor, it was always just a couple of streets away.

Sex was not a topic for general conversation. Certainly not one for discussion round the family dinner table. I can still instantly recall the shudder of embarrassment whenever I played 'Time' on *Aladdin Sane*, in the absolute sure knowledge that at the very moment Bowie reached the line 'Time . . . falls wanking to the floor' my mum would pop her head round the door and breezily announce: '*À table!*'

The sex education offered as an official part of the syllabus at school was called 'human biology', which seemed to involve discussing female and male organs in highly uncomfortable detail, and with the teacher blushing fit to burst (nowadays the kids probably sit the teachers down and explain shagging to *them*).

Unofficial briefings came in the playground or behind the bike sheds, from some kid whose brother claimed to have seen *Last Tango in Paris*, a couple of excessively dog-eared copies of *Fiesta* and some half-remembered glimpse of the bearded bloke in *The Joy of Sex* hard at it with his lady friend. We also tuned in to Capital Radio each Wednesday night, when Anna Raeburn and the Capital Doctor would engage in some alarmingly frank discussions involving one or more Dalmatians and, believe me, this wasn't Disney. Not bombarded with sex by the media – or not overtly at any rate – in the way we are today, this was all hair-raisingly frank.

Puberty involved incessant questions from school chums about how many gallons of 'man juice' one had produced. (On the menu of sexual euphemism this has probably now been renamed *jus d'homme*.) We stood in awe of the one gilded youth in the year above, who – it was strongly rumoured – had actually 'done it', and looked somewhat different as a result, at least to our innocent eyes.

When the opportunity finally came for the rest of us to 'do it' with a real live girl – rather than the fantasy figures of Sylvia Kristel of *Emmanuelle*, or even, dare I admit it, the Angels from *Captain Scarlet* (wooden puppets, I know, but damn sexy wooden puppets all the same) – it was still a mystery. But that was fun. Exploring the possibilities was an exciting journey, like discovering the source of the Niger fumble by fumble. When you finally got there and worked out what sex was really all about, the journey had been yours and yours alone – though obviously, or hopefully, not entirely alone at the vital moments.

John Inman or Biggins

Gay icons

8 September 1972 The pilot show of *Are You Being Served?* airs on BBC TV, the first outing for John Inman as Mr Humphries, and his catchphrase 'I'm free!'

My gran's generation would never accept that Mr Humphries – or Liberace, or Frankie Howerd, for that matter – was gay. 'Gay' was not a word they had ever used or even understood. 'Gay? No, love, he's just very happy.' For her generation, stereotypical camp characters were something straight out of musical hall, like Danny La Rue or Mrs Slocombe's 'pussy' jokes.

Camp was still very much alive in the 1970s. It was an odd thing. There was heterosexual, masculine camp: Leslie Phillips, cravat, toothbrush moustache, 'Ding dong!', or Terry-Thomas (the voice of Sir Hiss in the Disney version of *Robin Hood*), same moustache, same cravat, same drawl, same kind of maverick from the RAF, ready to scramble in their Lloyd Loom chairs.

And there was homosexual camp. Larry Grayson was the high priest of high camp, along with his imaginary friends Slack Alice, Apricot Lil and Everard (how many of the audience missed that double entendre?). Weirdly, in a covert time when high-profile stars never outed themselves, here was Larry on prime-time Saturday evening TV, hosting *The Generation Game* with Isla St Clair and mincing for England.

The advent of AIDS, that ridiculous 'gay disease' business, the outing of Rock Hudson, all started a huge ground shift. The world moved on. Covert became overt. Now Graham Norton can go where no mainstream presenter ever dared before, and revel in the freedom he has. And Christopher Biggins can win *I'm a Celebrity* . . . with his partner Neil there to welcome him out of the jungle. Thank God for all that change. But good old Biggins is living proof that camp has never gone away, and the nation still loves it.

Here's a little-known Glenister family fact. My uncle Colin Clews used to produce Larry Grayson – Larry always referred to him on air as 'Flash' Clews – and he and my auntie Joy were later invited to stay at Liberace's home in the States. Everything in the house, from the bedside tables to the ashtrays, was shaped like a piano. Even the piano . . .

Alf Garnett or Gene Hunt

Crusty geezers

26 December 1972 A classic comedy moment: Warren Mitchell as Alf Garnett in *Till Death Us Do Part*'s Christmas special argues that Jesus was English before conceding, 'Well, he might have been a bit Jewish on his father's side.'

He was one of the greatest comic creations ever: Johnny Speight's Alf Garnett. Here was a character who on the surface, and for anyone who couldn't be bothered to look a few inches beneath that surface, was a racist, sexist small-minded little Englander, full of pent-up prejudices and grievances. But Johnny Speight was too fine a writer to be that simplistic. Alf was not the Victor Meldrew of the National Front. There were deeper currents within him, confusions and puzzlements that reflected what was churning inside the British nation's psyche at the time.

It's amazing, really, that *Till Death Us Do Part* found a place in the mainstream schedules. Today's programme planners would tuck it away in some murky corner of the digital cupboard and see if it worked. In the 1970s there were – and isn't it astonishing to think about this, too? – only three channels that a programme like this could appear on. But there on BBC1, just after the watershed, was Alf – a fantastic portrayal by Warren Mitchell – with

Dandy Nichols, Una Stubbs (pre-*Give Us a Clue*) and the 'randy Scouse git' (Tony Booth, Tony Blair's future father-in-law) all pushing the edges of comedy with grit and verve. Compared to the *Till Death* . . . scripts, sitcoms that sat vaguely within the same area wielded much blunter bludgeons – *Love Thy Neighbour*, or later *Mind Your Language*, with its fantastically unimaginative European stereotypes.

There's a bit of Alf in DCI Gene Hunt. When I was offered the role of Hunt in *Life on Mars*, we all thought he was a pretty unpleasant character, simply representing an age when dinosaurs walked the beat. But as the series evolved we realised that, like Alf, this was a much more complex character who told us a lot more about what's changed in society over the last thirty years than about life in 1973. I have never had to defend Gene – if anything, I've had to criticise him because he has been embraced so fully, good and bad points. Gene is a big fan of Westerns: there's a poster of *The Good, the Bad and the Ugly* on the wall of his office. When he's asked which one he is, he says, 'I'm all three'.

One of the interesting things about Gene is that at a time when everyone, from the G8 summit outwards, hides behind weasel words and political–commercial verbiage, he talks the talk, says what nobody else dares to say. For example, there's the scene where the team is setting up a sting by pretending to be the staff in a post office. Gene's checking out the lads, making sure their weapons are ready. In walks WPC Cartwright. 'I haven't received any firearms training, sir,' she says. And what does Gene reply? 'You see, this is why birds and CID don't mix. You give a bloke a gun, it's a dream come true. You give a girl one, she moans it doesn't go with her dress. Now start behaving like a detective and show some balls . . .'

Routemaster or bendy bus

Road transport

20 May 1973 The final episode of *On the Buses*, starring Reg Varney as Stan Butler, and Stephen Lewis as Cyril 'Blakey' Blake – 'I 'ate you, Butler'.

Public transport seems to be much the same as ever, notwithstanding all the endless announcements of additional spending and improved services. Despite the statistics that are meant to prove the opposite, trains are still often late, crowded and dirty, London's roads are as clogged as ever, regardless of the congestion charge, and the buses are even more of a pain. They may always have arrived in convoy, but at least there was a conductor to chivvy people along, East End clippies keeping up their chirpy banter. With the conductors banished and the drivers encased in a protective cell, small wonder that travelling on a bus has turned into playing Russian roulette with the knife boys and the loons.

Routemaster buses, for the experienced, were a joy, hanging on the pole and nipping off when and where you wanted, without a jobsworth haranguing you or invoking the Health and Safety regulations, and plenty of room for prams and pushchairs. I really don't like the bendy buses, which must have squashed far more people than were ever at risk of falling off a Routemaster. They were designed for grid systems like they have in the States or Sweden, with plenty of room to turn corners, not for trolling up and down the narrow streets of antiquated city centres. That's the problem: our infrastructure is Victorian and it's creaking at the joints. When Jimmy Savile told us 'This is the age . . . of the train!', he must have been thinking of the 1870s, not the 1970s. Try and fix that, Jimbo!

Steve McQueen or Lee McQueen

A man's man

31 August 1973 Steve McQueen marries Ali McGraw, star of *Love Story*, and his co-star in *Getaway*. McGraw had left her husband, legendary film producer Robert Evans, for the King of Cool. The marriage lasted five years.

The first time I saw Steve McQueen on screen was one of those bank holidays when *The Great Escape* was shown for the first time on British TV, even though the movie had been released well over ten years earlier. In this era, if you missed a film when it did the rounds of the cinemas, that was pretty much it – pre-*video*, let alone pre-DVD. So whenever a film was broadcast on TV it was a major event: *Dr No*; *The Great Escape* – fab. Five-minute fragments of Disney cartoons were carefully doled out on *Disneytime*, hosted by the likes of Rolf Harris, the Goodies or Rod Hull and Emu, first just at Christmas and later on all the big bank holidays.

So there I was, watching Steve McQueen as Captain Virgil Hilts, working his magic, thumping the baseball against the wall of the cooler, gunning his motorbike to try to clear the border fence.

Steve was the Cooler King, cool incarnate, his blue sweat top customised, brown leather flying jacket. The man who'd starred in *Bullitt* driving his Mustang through the streets of San Francisco, a great city, being chased by Napoleon Solo – what's not to get hooked on? And then there was *The Towering Inferno*, released in 1974 but filmed in 1973 (the year the Twin Towers were officially opened). Paul Newman and McQueen vied for top billing. Famously, McQueen only agreed to do the film if he was given precisely the same number of lines as Newman. Then there was his poignant final appearance in *The Hunter*, just before cancer brought him down at the absurdly young age of fifty.

Now here's an extraordinary thing. I have never met, to my knowledge, anyone called McQueen. But there are at least four famous McQueens. Must be something in the gene pool of the Clan McQueen, because their presence punctuates the last half century in a roller-coaster of entertainment value.

It began with Steve, *the* man, even if the biographies say he was not quite as decent a guy as I'd like to think – but few idols are. Then there was Gordon McQueen, part of the uncompromising Leeds United team of the mid-'70s, a gangly central defender with huge red hair, who said, when he joined Man U in 1978, 'Ask all the players in the country which club they would like to join and 99 per cent would say Manchester United. The other 1 per cent would be liars.' Gordon retired in 1985, but the McQueen mantle was taken up by Alexander, a chap who makes clothes, or so I'm told (you'll gather I'm not an habitué of the catwalks).

And now the latest of this particular lineage is Lee

McQueen, the Apprentice of 2008, who may already have used up his fifteen minutes of fame. Here is a man refreshingly free of corporate speak, whose ideal recipient for the aftershave he cooked up for Sir Alan Sugar was 'a bloke who shaves his bollocks' – thanks for sharing, Lee – and who was not above falsifying his CV. (Did you ever see my starring role in *The Great Escape*, by the way?) Mind you, anyone who agrees to appear on a reality show is always going to be at the mercy of those lovely folk in the edit suite, and we'd all end up, whatever we imagine, looking like hideously ambitious nutters – apart from Sir Alan, who has all the best lines.

So we've travelled from the King of Cool to a geezer whose party piece is a reverse pterodactyl impression. Come on you McQueens. Get procreating and let's buck the trend.

Green Shield stamps or Air Miles

Collecting

12 October 1973 In the Genesis track 'Dancing with the Moonlight Knight', from *Selling England by the Pound*, the lyrics refer to 'Knights of the Green Shield', the only known reference to Green Shield stamps in the rock canon.

There must be some basic human urge, a throwback to hunter–gatherer days, that requires us to collect. The urge is still as strong as ever, though the objects we collect have changed.

My memories are of collecting cigarette cards, each with an illustration on the front and a paragraph of information on the back that had been slipped behind the silver foil in a pack of fags. Cigarettes may have damaged your health but you could always console yourself that you'd forever be able to name all the nation's kings and queens. To fill the card books so thoughtfully provided by the tobacco companies on different themes – from great characters in history to racing cars – required demanding that all my relatives chainsmoke themselves stupid like a pack of bea-gles. The Typhoo Tea cards worked on the same principle, only this time the family risked a tannin overdose.

Every four years, there were the petrol stations' World Cup coins and all year round the endless sets of tumblers and wine glasses to collect. I also dabbled in stamp collecting through my Saturday job with a local philatelist. The autograph book had to be filled, and the cereal packets rummaged through to find a tiny piece of plastic. Model soldiers, Panini stickers, odd-shaped rubbers – the options were endless: other kids would be stashing away anything from Top Trumps to trolls, gonks to Smurfs, and plastic farm animals to Sylvanian family wildlife. And in any quiet time, the Green Shield stamps from the mini-mart had to be carefully gummed into their bulging booklets.

On and on it went. Now it's *High School Musical* stickers, used phone cards, Air Miles, supermarket loyalty points that you will never redeem (although supermarkets have cannily and gratefully gleaned all your personal details and shopping habits). In the midst of all this collecting and cataloguing, it's getting harder and harder to collect my bleedin' thoughts!

Nimble or spelt

Bread of life

November 1973 Ridley Scott, no less, films the 'Boy and his Bike' Hovis ad in Shaftesbury, Dorset, which from then on will always be evoked by the strains of Dvořák's *New World Symphony*.

I was too young to be a flower child, but I was definitely a flour child. Great chunks of crusty bread, proper doorstep sandwiches, and packets of bread so gleamingly white the slices must have had cosmetic dentistry. Wonderloaf, as absorbent as any kitchen towel, perfect for cleaning up every last drop of gravy from the dinner plate. No need for a dishwasher! Just get your dad.

The only alternative to white bread was Hovis – which sounded healthy, though who knows why that poor kid had to push his bike up a vertiginous hill with a brass band playing in the background. Imagine shooting that ad nowadays. The kid would have his agent on the phone straight away – 'No way he's walking up that hill for a reshoot.'

The 'lighter' option was Nimble, and they had another great ad. The balloon drifting across open countryside. And two catchy little numbers. 'She flies like a bird through the sky-y-y/She flies like a bird and I wish that she were mine.' And the other: 'Would you like to ride in my beautiful, my beautiful balloon?' Now here's a perfect pub-quiz question. Can you name the two songs and the groups who originally sang them? (Answers below!) Those ads merge in my mind with 'I'd like to teach the world to sing', probably because the shiny, happy people singing it on the hilltop were filmed from a balloon. Another great song, shame about the corporate product. I once read that the New Seekers, two cute girls, geeky bass player, two good-looking dudes, ended up having to sing the song so often that one of the girls was physically sick each time they went back on stage for the encore.

If you wanted something healthy, you had to go to the 'health food shop', usually Holland & Barrett, which emitted a vaguely hippyish aroma of dried fruits mixed with Tartex spread and joss sticks. These were the days when non-meat-eaters had to settle for nut cutlets at Christmas and only ever got offered salad as the 'vegetarian option'. Not so these days. Health food is everywhere now. And the humble loaf of bread? Whenever you nip into the local baker's – or the *'artisan de pain'* as he doubtless prefers to be called – there's too much choice: all that spelt, sourdough, cholla, multi-grain, poppy seed, pumpernickel or markouk. And there's no chance of a nice bit of Wonderloaf or some plain white. Kids nowadays can forget coming home from school, grabbing a crust of white bread, a can of Cresta, a bowl of butterscotch Angel Delight, and plonking themselves down to watch *Scooby-Doo*. The health police will have 'em.

Answer: 'I Can't Let Maggie Go' by Honeybus and 'Up, Up and Away' by the Fifth Dimension. Both were re-recorded specially for the ads. Download them now!

Police 5 or *Crimewatch*

DIY detection

1 February 1974 Jack Slipper, 'Slipper of the Yard', finally tracks down and arrests Great Train Robber Ronnie Biggs in Rio de Janeiro, but is thwarted by Brazil's extradition regulations. Biggs revels in the celebrity.

The perfect Sunday television schedule, *circa* 1975, went like this. In the morning there was *Aquarius*, which opened with Emerson, Lake & Palmer doing a bit of prog rock toccata work. The programme itself was full of evangelical hippies, or so it seemed, and was followed by Brian Walden's *Weekend World*, which was shit if you were twelve, so that was a signal for us to bunk off for lunch. The post-prandial entertainment started hotting up when, just before *The Big Match*, there was a great warm-up act with Shaw Taylor presenting *Police 5*. All ITV, you'll notice – the BBC shows kicked in later with *Ski Sunday*.

I got to meet Shaw recently when he came and did a cameo, as himself, in *Ashes to Ashes*. He was still as calm and unflappable as ever, the voice of reassurance, and it was a joy to hear him deliver that great pay-off, which I think he only ever used on *Junior Police 5* during the week – 'Keep 'em peeled'. Perfect choice of words. This was interactive TV in its infancy, before DNA testing and hi-tech forensics, a chance to phone in to the television station and nail a villain (we can't call them villains any more – they're 'behaviourally challenged socially dys-functional victims'). We spent the rest of the week with eyes peeled in eager anticipation, though the primitive photo-fits they showed could have been absolutely any-body. (Your dad?)

After Shaw Taylor came Nick Ross – as professional and reassuring as his predecessor – with Sue Cook (and later Jill Dando, of course) on *Crimewatch*. Now the studios are chock-full of police working the phones, while the coppers with speaking parts seem to have been media-trained to within an inch of their lives. It's all light years away from the tongue-tied plods Shaw used to wheel on. I'm waiting for *Police Idol* to be commissioned, when we can pick the next glamorous DC to present the CCTV footage. Blimey, even the traffic cops in those reality car-chase shows con-stantly mug for the cameras. They've probably all got agents now. Soon us actors will have to form a vigilante squad and swap jobs with them all.

One little footnote. Weekend TV for me was special, because in the London area Friday night changed from Thames TV (with its Tower Bridge logo) to LWT, London Weekend Television, at 7 p.m. Hey, hey, it's the weekend, it's official, it's right there in the name. Each of the regional ITV companies' logos provoked a different response. ATV – it's bound to be *Crossroads*. Granada – *Corrie*. That spinning silver knight from Anglia – 'Now, from Norwich, it's the quiz of the week' – *Sale of the*

Century. Southern – *How!* with the crack team of Fred Dinenage, countryman Jack Hargreaves, that egghead bloke and mumsy Bunty James. Lovely.

The Liver Birds or Sex and the City

City girls

3 April 1974 The last episode of *The Liver Birds* pairing Polly James as Beryl and Nerys Hughes as Sandra. Beryl left to get married and Carol (Elizabeth Estensen) moved in for the next series.

There are some theme tunes you can never forget. The piccolos at the start of *Some Mothers Do 'Ave 'Em*, a Ronnie Hazlehurst masterpiece, playing a tune that in Morse code spells out the title of the show. Inspired. Try whistling it without laughing at some stage.

Whatever Happened to the Likely Lads?, with its jaunty poignancy ('the only thing to look forward to's the past'). *Van Der Valk*, pure gold. Interesting that when *The Office* wanted a dose of poignancy for its theme, they chose the melancholic strains of 'Handbags and Gladrags', the Mike d'Abo song that Rod Stewart made famous.

And then there was *The Liver Birds* and its whistling theme tune. Roger Whittaker was clearly more influential than I realised, or the BBC budget was so tight that they were cutting back on the woodwind section. I always hoped that John Lennon might have been the whistler, and Ringo the guy who asks, 'You dancin'?', but now I know it was the Scaffold, including Macca's brother Mike McGear.

Ah, the Liver Birds. The female equivalents of the Likely Lads, Terry and Bob. Polly James perky as Beryl (the Terry role); Nerys Hughes quieter, less daring (the Bob equivalent). Pauline Collins was Polly James's original flatmate for the first series, but I never saw her in it. Nerys and Polly were the ones for me.

That was a golden age of bedsit sitcoms: Richard O'Sullivan shacked up – dream on – with Paula Wilcox and Sally Thomsett in *Man About the House*; Rigsby trying to rule the roost in *Rising Damp*. They set up a long tradition of flat-sharing shows: from Rik Mayall, Ade Edmondson and co. in *The Young Ones* to *Men Behaving Badly* and on through to *Friends*, *Pulling*, *Peep Show* and doubtless beyond.

But I've always had a soft spot for *The Liver Birds*. There was a sweet innocence about Carla Lane's scripts, and in the way Sandra and Beryl played off each other. Although they were always up for scouting for talent, they were really quite coy, and a quick snog was the best a suitor could hope for, certainly on screen, when the studio audience, all lovely old dears, would go 'oooh' in unison. Their extended families, including Mollie Sugden as Sandra's snobby mum, were part of the show too, like the live-in families in *Till Death Us Do Part* and *On the Buses*. That close-knit nuclear family feel is getting rarer by the day.

I know the 'urban girls go for it' of *Sex and the City* was hugely popular, but do girls really only talk about shopping and fucking? (And the sex was definitely a sideline to the shopping.) Unlike *The Liver Birds*, there was no sense of family – did these women have parents? I know they were meant to be single and footloose, but not orphans. The world of Carrie, Samantha and the others was an exclusive one – and a lot of us weren't invited. Whereas *The Liver Birds* was never just a girl thing, just the tale of the adventures of two girls, two real girls you might conceivably bump into in the local pub, who shared a flat in Liverpool. As simple and exquisitely balanced as 'You dancin'? You askin'? I'm askin'. I'm dancin'. . .'

Cresta or smoothie

Soft drinks

22 June 1974 A silver award at the International Advertising Festival for R. White's 'Secret Lemonade Drinker' ad, featuring a man in striped pyjamas raiding the fridge at night – Elvis Costello's dad wrote and sang the song (with his son on backing vocals).

The history of the carbonated drink is long and illustrious, and has spawned some of the finest TV ads known to man . . . or known to this man, at least.

Right up there in pole position has to be Cresta. It was *seriously* frothy, man! And that polar bear with his shades, the funky reprobate brother of the Glacier Mints bear. Five fruity flavours – though the pink strawberry bore possibly the most tenuous of connections to the kind of strawberry you put in your punnet at the pick-your-own. I guess the Trades Descriptions Act was still in its infancy. This stuff blew your head off.

Tizer – what the hell taste was that meant to be? No Irn Bru in those days for London lads like me – it had to be bussed in. Later, when you could get it down south, I was at drama school: my flatmate Gordon Anderson, who was from Leeds, told me it never tasted the same south of Watford.

In the wake of the milk float and the ice-cream van came the Corona van, that champion of the pre-Tango fizzy orange parade – its only real rival Fanta. Another great ad too, with the 'every bubble's passed its fizzical' line. And R. White's lemonade – legendary. I never had much time for cream soda, or cherryade, just as later I turned up my nose – and still do – at Perrier and Evian. Water in a bottle – use the bloody tap (I'm glad to see I've recently been proved right!). And an honourable mention for the Sodastream, that essential stand-by of the suave '70s drinks party, with its little gas canister. It was a brave try, though the puny bubbles disappeared by the time your glass reached your mouth.

So there we all were, guzzling sugar-rich drinks by the jeroboam. Cocaine for kids. We must have been on a permanent sugar high. Around sports day some parents used to slip their kids a tablet of Dextrosol glucose. On top of a bottle of Cresta the combination was lethal. Even Ben Johnson would have said no. Still, it kept the dental profession ticking over.

And if you were sick you could always look forward to the crinkly sound of the orange cellophane on the Lucozade bottle.

The nasty-things-free smoothies of today are pitched as healthy alternatives to what we used to pour down our throats, and it's hard to lay your hands legally on a can of anything with the heady rush of Cresta, or of Coke boiled up with an aspirin, which was – so the rumour at school went – able to give you the ultimate high, but probably just gave you the ultimate headache.

Cresta or smoothie

Holidays in France added the exotic flavour of Orangina – now available everywhere in the UK, of course, but then *très* French. And there was a lemonade you could get in French supermarkets with the wonderful name of Pschitt. As the man said, 'Is it just me, or is everything still Pschitt?'

Watergate or Kittygate
Scandals

8 August 1974 Richard Milhous Nixon, thirty-seventh president of the United States of America, announces his resignation in the fallout from Watergate. 'I have never been a quitter,' he tells the nation, foreshadowing Peter Mandelson.

Nixon resigning. That was a proper stand-up scandal. Corruption in the heart of the White House. Lies in the Oval Office. Fearless journalists digging and digging. Mysterious trysts with Deep Throat. A president brought to justice. It had to be the real thing – Dustin Hoffman and Robert Redford were drafted in for the movie. A defining moment for the 1970s. And kudos to David Frost for squeezing a sort of confession out of the old politico. You know, Nixon was so hangdog, I almost felt sorry for him, in my eleven-year-old ignorance.

Clinton not resigning. That was not a proper stand-up scandal. Well, part of it was standing up. But no, no, no. Not a fifty-something geezer caught with his trousers down with a twenty-year-old muffin, and playing president and intern with a cigar. Sorry, Bill, that's a pathetic excuse for a scandal.

And guess what everyone called it: Monicagate (or Tailgate, or Zippergate) . . . very imaginative. The value of that Something-gate cliché has gone down faster than ol' Slick Willie ever did. Look at the evidence. Camillagate. The heir to the throne is eavesdropped comparing himself to the future Duchess of Cornwall's tampon. Bloody hell! I know he didn't plan on being overheard, but Charles – while you may be spot on when it comes to organic farming and architecture – that was just a little bit weird. I think I'd rather be Bill's cigar. No, on second thoughts, let's not go there.

But if Camillagate was a new low, then Kittygate was a further step down. I know in the new post-phone-in scam, super-transparent, squeaky-clean BBC all the execs are running around in a state of complete panic, but frankly who cares if the new *Blue Peter* cat is called Cock or Socks or whatever? And then, to add insult to injury, they dubbed it Kittygate. That's not a scandal; it's just sad.

Wikipedia has a list of forty-nine 'widely recognised' scandals with a -gate suffix. Everything's a scandal in the 24/7 news climate. Editors are desperate to fill the endless hours on Sky News and News 24, and pad out the tabloids. Every minor cock-up, off-message ministerial remark or sexual peccadillo is given the full Watergate treatment. And amid all that smoke, the real scandals – maybe, let's say, invading a country on the basis of some completely spurious intelligence; a ridiculous idea, I know – slide on by with no one resigning, nobody even holding their hand up and saying, 'Whoops, sorry, screwed that up,' just everybody cruising on regardless. Fudge, fudge and more fudge. But luckily not a finger of fudge, otherwise we might be giving a future president of the United States ideas.

———

Emmanuelle or Films for Fellas

Soft-core porn

20 September 1974 Emmanuelle is released in the UK, with Sylvia Kristel in the title role. 'X was never like this', shouted the tagline. Suzanne Danielle plays the lead role in *Carry On Emmannuelle* four years later.

Soft-core porn was furtive, exciting, a little bit scary, embarrassing. There was a real flush of fear involved in reaching up to the top shelf, trying to hide *Fiesta* from view inside a copy of *Shoot!*, just in case the next-door neighbours had popped into the same newsagent's, and hoping that your voice wouldn't break when you spoke to the shopkeeper.

It was all pretty tame stuff. The films we might catch a glimpse of were romps – *Emmanuelle*, Robin Askwith in the *Confessions of . . .* series (*Window Cleaner*, *Pop Performer*, *Driving Instructor*, *Chartered Accountant* – OK, they never got round to making that last one), a raunchier version of the *Carry On . . .* series with its big breast jokes, Sid James going 'yak yak yak', Bernie Bresslaw ('Cor, blimey, Sid') and Kenneth Connor's 'phwoarr'.

The magazines were not much more explicit. *Playboy*, *Park Lane*, *Penthouse* and *Mayfair* were the sorts of publications, as their names suggested, that a dashing blade at his gentleman's club – Jason King, for example – might openly read. Even the scuzzier end was ridiculously amateur, especially the Readers' Wives sections, where hirsute was the predominant look. No Brazilians there . . . more the whole Amazonian rainforest. For girls, sitting at the back of the classroom during double chemistry and passing round books by Judy Blume was as risqué as it got.

So it was a shock when in one of my first jobs a package arrived in the morning mail that contained a full-on set of photos featuring two swinging couples hard at it, sent by one of the couples to the other, but to the wrong address. This was the real thing – eye-opening stuff in such sweet, innocent days. Hard-core existed out there somewhere – and had done since the twisted-up Victorian days and before – but you had to go out of your way to track it down: to a bloke offering dodgy Super-8 movies, or swishing through the bead curtains to enter dank 'adult' shops in Soho. Today, flick through the Freeview channels after the watershed or enter certain keywords into Google and you can see whatever you like, whenever you like. It's too easy. Too much access, not enough mystery.

Magpie or (still) *Blue Peter*
Kids' TV

15 October 1974 The *Magpie* team of Susan Stranks, Mick Robertson and Douglas Rae gets a shake-up when Jenny Hanley replaces Stranks.

One of the defining choices any '70s kid had to make – up there with plumping for Borg or McEnroe, Arsenal or Spurs – was between *Blue Peter* and *Magpie*. I ended up being a defector, having started off firmly in the *Blue Peter* camp. Susan Stranks had always seemed a bit too Headmistress to tempt me across. Then the hot new Head Girl arrived on the scene in the form of Jenny Hanley. She was a former Bond girl, after all (appearing in *On Her Majesty's Secret Service*), and the rosy cheeks of Lesley Judd were no match.

One edition of *Blue Peter* has stayed with me, though, when Lesley couldn't appear in the studio because she'd been struck down with chickenpox or mumps. So the chaps, Peter Purves and John Noakes, headed out to visit her at home, where she was propped up in bed, virtually comatose, barely able to speak. Lesley soldiered on gamely, displaying the kind of end-of-Empire spirit that was at the core of *Blue Peter*. It wouldn't have happened on *Magpie*. If Jenny Hanley had been laid low, Mick

Robertson – Brian May's long-lost brother – probably would have rolled her a herbal fag and told her to stay mellow.

So I left behind the cosy world of guide dogs, tortoises and incontinent elephants for an altogether edgier environment and jumped ship from the cheery hornpipe of *Blue Peter* to the rockier, darker theme tune of 'One for sorrow, two for joy', and the mystery of a secret never to be told. Never did learn what it was.

I can hear the whirring of a Betamax machine powering up. What programmes are flickering across the old retinas? *Crackerjack* – Peter Glaze and Leslie Crowther on Friday afternoons, with the *Crackerjack* pencil as coveted as the *Blue Peter* badge (very much the prefect's badge) or later the *Blankety-Blank* chequebook and pen or *3-2-1*'s Dusty Bin.

On *Crackerjack*'s Double or Drop quiz, the contestants had to stand there holding the prizes – and cabbages if they gave the wrong answer – teetering in their arms until they couldn't carry any more. That was later replaced by gunge, lots of it, still a staple part of children's TV, although – thanks to Health and Safety – the kids who get gunged are equipped with the kind of goggles and protective clothing that Red Adair would have found handy for putting out oil-rig blazes.

Home-produced dramas: *Double Deckers* and *The Freewheelers*. Imported dramas: *White Horses* ('snowy white horses' to fuel the same horse passion engendered by *Follyfoot*, *Black Beauty* and *Champion the Wonder Horse*), *Skippy*, *Daktari*, *Robinson Crusoe* and *Belle and Sebastien* –

Pyrenean mountain dog takes on the might of the Nazi hordes! Entertainment from the US of A: *Banana Splits*, *The Partridge Family* and the *Osmonds* cartoon on Saturday mornings, *Wacky Races* and – here's an obscure one – *Wait Till Your Father Gets Home*. By the late '70s, though, the crucial Saturday morning viewing was coming from the Midlands in the form of *Tiswas* – Chris Tarrant, Sally James, Lenny Henry, Bob Carolgees and Spit the Dog – who were in direct competition with Noel Edmonds and Cheggers on *Swap Shop*.

On weekday evenings, as children's TV shut down just before the news, the five-minute animated shorts cycled round, a different one for each day. *The Wombles* wombled free, *The Clangers* made absolute sense through a swanee whistle. We were exposed to the adventures of *Captain Pugwash* and *Noggin the Nog*, the whimsy of *Hector's House* or *The Herbs* and the psychedelic trips of *Crystal Tipps and Alistair*. And the daddy of them all, *The Magic Roundabout*, with Emma Thompson's dad Eric's voice-over and the coolest kids' character in history, Dylan.

As a dad, I'm now tuned in to *Raven* or *Hider in the House*, and trying to avoid the option of CBeebies, CITV or any of the other perma-kids' channels as a convenient nanny. Thirty years hence, I wonder if those shows will produce such a warm retrospective glow.

Oh, and before we return to the Test Card, I must mention *Camberwick Green*. When John Simm and I were turned into *Camberwick Green* characters for *Life on Mars*, I can tell you now, it was a highlight of both our lives . . .

Pomagne or alcopops

Underage drinking

22 February 1975 Drew Barrymore is born. By the age of seven she is starring as Gertie in *E.T.*, by the age of nine she is drinking and gets a reputation as Hollywood's youngest alcoholic.

At a time when the scourge of teenage binge drinking is high on the political agenda, I shall keep my memories of underage drinking as short and sharp as a tequila slammer poured down the throat. Suffice to say that there has always been underage drinking. But when I was underage the phenomenon hadn't been labelled, or institutionalised, or targeted by branding consultants. There were no alcopops handily displayed in the local corner shop. But there was plenty of Top Deck shandy – about 99 per cent lemonade, 1 per cent lager, from memory – and my drink of choice, Pomagne, a sparkling sham-pagne derived from some kind of fruit, possibly pears, that to an uneducated teenage palate was as fine a libation as vintage champagne. And imbibed in vast quantities it could certainly make you throw up just as quickly.

New Faces **or** *Britain's Got Talent*

Talent shows

27 July 1975 Marti Caine wins the All Winners Gala Final of *New Faces*, beating both Lenny Henry and Victoria Wood. Her prize is a chance to perform at the MGM Grand in Las Vegas.

On Saturday evenings, along with my friends from school, I used to sing a nifty variation of the *New Faces* theme tune. The original version accompanying the little cartoon busker on the show's opening titles was performed by Carl Wayne, once of the Move – the band whose 'Flowers in the Rain' was the first track ever played on Radio One. 'You're a star, superstar', Carl would sing, and my bunch of mates would chorus, 'Wearing knickers and a fuckin' bra'. Yep, I was an urbane sophisticate even then.

As a talent show, *New Faces* seemed to us more credible than *Opportunity Knocks*. Hughie Green harked back to an earlier age, to *Double Your Money* and Monica Rose, somehow very '60s. And the winning acts were schmaltzier: Bobby Crush, Lena Zavaroni and Peters and Lee, though we all gave kudos to Les Dawson, and my Welsh blood won't let me hear a word said against Mary Hopkin or Max Boyce.

It can't have been the *New Faces* set that gave the show credibility, though: a few sheets of plywood and a bit of balsa tarted up with some sparkle and stars. And the scoring system was hardly hi-tech. *Opportunity Knocks* had boasted the 'clapometer', a gauge of audience reaction which never seemed to bear the slightest relationship to the level of applause. The *New Faces* equivalent was a scoreboard simply adding up marks for Presentation, Content and the all-important Star Quality, but it still launched the careers of Victoria Wood, Les Dennis and Lenny Henry.

The big difference between *New Faces* and *Britain's Got Talent* was that a panel of judges rather than the public made the decision. And the judges always included the 'hard man', an industry insider who wasted no time pulling punches, usually Tony Hatch, the songwriter, or Mickie Most, the boss of RAK Records and the guy behind Suzi Quatro, Sweet and Mud. It made the whole show much more gladiatorial, although they softened the blows slightly by surrounding the tough talkers with a genial showbiz veteran like Arthur Askey, Lionel Blair or Ted Ray, an MOR DJ, perhaps Ed 'Stewpot' Stewart or Alan 'Fluff' Freeman, and a cute female entertainer such as Una Stubbs or Lynsey 'No Honestly' De Paul. I can almost hear the production team's wish-list – an old geezer, a platter spinner for the kids and a dolly bird.

Roll on thirty years. Extract the remote from your kid's fearsome grip (who is probably watching, stony-faced, the Chuckle Brothers, still going after winning *New Faces* in 1974) and you can catch . . . *Britain's Got Talent*. Featuring one hard man/industry insider, a.k.a. Mr Cowell, cloned from Tony H and Mickie M; an apparently genial twat in the form of Piers Morgan; and Amanda Holden. No difference at all. Apart from whether in three decades' time anyone other than their mums will be able to recall who won. And I mean that most sincerely, folks . . .

Clacton or CenterParcs

Great British holidays

30 September 1975 Brighton's famous Eugenius Birch-designed West Pier, a symbol of the great British seaside holiday, is closed for safety reasons. Its tattered skeletal remains linger off the beach for decades more.

My golf handicap can always do with a little extra work, but if I ever put in a really good round I can't help thinking that it's thanks to the groundwork I laid thirty years ago on some of the great crazy golf courses along the British coastline. I don't know whether Tiger ever had the pleasure of getting a golf ball across a ramp and through a tiny door at the bottom of a windmill, but if he'd like to go head to head I reckon I could take him down.

Crazy golf, at Clacton, Ventnor, Llandudno or Clee-thorpes, was part of the classic British seaside holiday. Through the '70s and '80s the lure of the Costa del Sol was making serious inroads into the numbers of British families heading to our coast, but for those of us who still made the trek to Minehead or Whitley Bay, all the essential ingredients could be found: Punch and Judy on the prom, toy yachts on sailing ponds, miniature steam railways reeking of coal smoke, Fawlty-esque B&B owners, beach huts and bandstands. And always those seafront shops

---

where we could spend our hard-saved pocket money on spinning windmills, sticks of rock, and all kinds of useless tat – as you still can.

The resorts with fine sandy beaches were great, naturally, but surely the pebble beach was more challenging. It took true British grit to wield a rubber mallet and try to hammer your family's windbreak into solid shingle in a vain attempt to defeat blasting northerly gales, though at least on those beaches there was no sand to infiltrate the packed lunches. We also respected the very highest degree of British reserve by learning how to change into our swimming cossies underneath a towel. My mum at one point bought a huge all-in-one towelling robe to make the process easier: like a vast cuddly tent, it threatened to engulf us while we struggled into dashing Speedos or tried to peel them off if we had ventured into the hypothermia-inducing waters.

When the rain came, we soldiered on. Or if it really got too much to bear, there were always the amusement arcades to fall back on. Come to think of it, if Tiger and I are tied after nine holes of crazy golf, I'd offer him sudden death on a Penny Falls machine any day or maybe some matchplay on the claw machine or the one-armed bandit.

The classic resorts have hung in there, one way or another. Southwold prides itself on offering an ozone-heavy whiff of the great seaside holiday days, while Newquay's reinvented itself as surf central. But things have often looked grim for all those great seaside towns which used to 'play the joker' with Stuart Hall and Eddie Waring on *It's a Knockout*, shortly before destroying pianos, picking eggs up with JCB diggers, or dressing up as penguins to carry buckets of water across slippery poles and spinning logs. (Try commissioning that show now and it would end up as a 'carefully executed, rigorously safety-checked game where everyone is ultimately a winner'.)

In places like Southport, Lytham St Anne's and Great Yarmouth, no sooner had Eddie and Stuart disappeared than yet more outside broadcast vans would arrive to set up *Seaside Special*. I was naïvely convinced, by the way, that all the dancers on *Seaside Special* must be going out with each other; otherwise, how could they all get so intimate on stage? After *Seaside Special*, the Radio One Roadshow would turn up to provide MOR entertainment and overfamiliar DJs.

My family headed most often to south Wales, where we had relatives. One of my mum's cousins had a caravan down there, at Llangennith on the Gower Peninsula. Magical holidays, in an era when we could and would roam across the sand dunes or trawl the rock pools all day long, improvising toboggans out of bits of cardboard to sledge down the dunes. Or we could simply buy a lilo and float dangerously out to sea.

I'm still a big fan of holidays in the UK, but I personally don't care much for the CenterParcs concept. I know it's supersafe – although it's a sad indictment of where we are now in terms of child safety that nobody dares risk letting their kids wander the dunes and rock pools out of sight any more. And there are fantastic activities for everybody in the family – you can't knock that. But everything pampered and protected under one roof, even if it is a natural canopy of forest trees, smacks of finding yourself trapped in an episode of *The Prisoner*. 'I am not a number! I am a free man!' (No, you're not, Dad. Now put on this protective body armour and let's go paintballing.')

The Galloping Gourmet or
The ****in' Ramsay

TV chefs

17 October 1975 First showing of the 'Gourmet Night' episode of *Fawlty Towers*: Basil's plan to impress Torquay society with a night of gastronomy goes horribly awry. The final line: 'Duck's off. Sorry!'

An Antipodean breath of fresh air, Graham Kerr, the Galloping Gourmet, bounded into our living room some-where around 1972. Previously the art of fine cooking had been the preserve of French chefs kitted out in toque and white coat, the elite of haute (and very haughty) cuisine, or Fanny Cradock, with her painted-on eyebrows and her husband, old stage-door Johnny, briskly marching viewers through her complicated, fussy recipes. It was all quite off-putting.

Then along came the convivial, elegant Kerr, born in the UK but who'd spent many years in New Zealand. A man who seemed to enjoy his cooking, helped by the occasional slurp of white wine. He had a great line in patter and banter, interacting with and chatting to the studio audience, and made the whole process sound fun. For the opening of the programme he hurdled a dining chair. At the end of every show, he would turn out the dish he'd been busily preparing on to a little round table for two, covered by a check tablecloth, choose a dinner partner from the audience and gallantly escort her (it was invariably a her) to the table to sample his creation, and then proceeded to re-enact a gastronomic orgasm over his own food. Modesty was not in Kerr's cupboard. Fantastic entertainment. Most of all the Galloping Gourmet sent out the message that cooking could be done by men other than the three-star professionals, and that if you were nifty with a skillet and a pair of oven gloves, your chances of pulling would be greatly enhanced. Revolutionary stuff.

When the Gourmet skipped off the schedules, his *bon viveur* style of cooking was taken over by the bow-tied Keith Floyd, who upped the wine intake to alarming degrees in *Floyd on Fish, . . . France*, etc. (or how about *Pink Floyd on Cooking? – Dark Side of the Spoon* and *Whisk You Were Here*). Keith's claret-guzzling, *Year in Provence* approach to cooking, the counterbalance to Delia Smith's eminently sensible style, eventually wilted under the strain, leaving the way open for spiky-quiffed Gary Rhodes and a new breed of younger, fitter cooks to force their way through the serving hatch. Jamie, Hugh, Gordon and Nigella all pounded their pestles alongside a revitalised Delia. So many cooking programmes, jostling for position with the relocation shows, the interior designers, the makeover artists – enough!

All of those programmes seem to have been heading in the direction of fierce confrontation, and Gordon Ramsay has always been in the vanguard on that score. Can you believe the Australian broadcasting authorities finally pulled the plug on *The F Word* because there was too much swearing? Well, fuck me, mate.

James Hunt or Lewis Hamilton

Formula One Brits

24 October 1975 In a rain-sodden Japanese Grand Prix, James Hunt manages to overcome a puncture and pit problems to claim third place, gaining four points and taking the Formula One Drivers' Championship by a single point from Niki Lauda.

After the great years of British Formula One drivers in the '50s and '60s – Stirling Moss, Mike Hawthorn, Jim Clark and Jackie Stewart – the numbers suddenly dropped off, although there were plenty of British racing teams. Most of all we needed a successor to the dash of Graham Hill, with his pencil moustache and flying scarf.

We got lucky with James Hunt, the ultimate playboy F1 champion. In the opening titles of *The Persuaders* there was a headline that read, 'Lord Brett Sinclair Wins Grand Prix'. Hunt was Roger Moore's Brett Sinclair incarnate, a maverick with a passion for speed and high-rolling risks. Hunt left his golden locks long and unkempt, had a taste for blonde totty, and gave the impression he had spent the night before every Grand Prix carousing at Annabel's and come straight to the circuit only after the club had closed in the early dawn. The guy must have refuelled on champagne, and rather than yet another bottle to celebrate a podium position, a whisky chaser might have been more appropriate. Needless to say, he was also a bloody good driver.

British Formula One champs have been few and far between since Hunt's triumph. Nigel Mansell, Damon Hill, and now the promise of Lewis Hamilton. F1 now is a very different sport from the one James Hunt knew. There's no cigarette sponsorship, of course, with the Marlboro and JPS Special days long gone. (Embassy also had to pack in their support of the World Snooker Championships. Previously the venue had been more Ashtray than Crucible, with Hurricane Higgins and Cliff Thorburn slugging it out in a fug of smoke and lager fumes.)

The risk factor in Formula One has been drastically reduced. It's now a battle between the engineers in the pit lane watching the tacho information and nursing their drivers through intricate calculations, taking the key decisions from the safety of their laptops. Meanwhile, the drivers train on PlayStation simulations of each track to build up muscle memory. The control and the planning have taken the thrill away – and the horrible truth is that F1 used to be far more exciting when there was the possibility of a major pile-up. The mavericks have been corralled in a lock-up garage and there's not a Graham Hill-style flying scarf in sight. Shame.

Cooking oil or factor 50

Climate change

3 July 1976 In the heatwave summer of '76, this is the hottest day, and one of the hottest on record, with temperatures reaching nearly 36°C (over 96°F) in Cheltenham.

Whenever there was a hint of sun in the 1970s, we'd be off to the coast like a shot, slapping on the Ambre Solaire – fantastic smell, by the way – as if it were cooking oil, basting tonight. Plonk down on to the beach and you'd be covered with a thick coating of sand, like a giant chicken Kiev, as you gently sizzled away and – especially on the Costa Brava – mutated into a giant lobster Thermidor.

Then we all got wise to the fact that this might not be such a brilliant idea, especially as the rising temperature of the globe threatens to turn Bognor Regis into Bondi Beach. Aussie-style, everybody's kids get slathered in sun factor so high it's in three digits, a kind of gungy white goose fat that was previously reserved for attempts to swim the Channel.

So how do you achieve that tanned look? Fake it. Later, in the 1980s, there was Duo Tan, and Sun-in, which made your hair go bright orange, so everyone looked like Cindy Lauper. Once, the only thing that orange was the floral wallpaper in your parents' bedroom. Suddenly everybody was sporting the Kia-Ora look. And now you can walk into a cubicle down the high street and be sprayed as if you were the garden fence getting its annual coating of creosote. The effect can be startling, but probably preferable to the old school of bright red Brits abroad – and definitely safer.

Jehovah's Witnesses or mobile upgrade

Cold-calling

23 July 1976 The cold-caller's anthem is released: 'Let 'Em In' by Paul McCartney and Wings – can you remember who was knocking at the door and who was ringing that bell? – with Sister Suzy, Brother John, Martin Luther, Phil and Don *et al.*

Time was when the only people who cold-called you had to come to your front door, especially if your family had been wise enough to go ex-directory. I'm not sure why, but going ex-directory was quite mysterious, as if your dad was actually a suburban 007, or your mum an undercover sleeper for the intelligence services.

One deft flick of the net curtains in the hall would provide enough warning. There were four main varieties of door-knockers and buzzer-ringers. (If you excluded the kids – and I include myself in that category – who rang the bell and ran away. Simple pleasures.) The earnest young men from the Jehovah's Witnesses took the inevitable snub with the patient, tolerant smile of people who expected to move on to an eternal paradise, and had a shrewd suspicion that our family wouldn't be joining them there. My good friend, the Lord Mendelson of Roehampton, patron of the arts, developed his own Jehovah's Witness-specific riposte whenever they called. 'Aren't you a little bit old', he'd ask, 'to have an imaginary friend?' Hot on their heels came the cheerful church regulars who once a year sold 'smiley faces', photos of grinning kids from the former colonies, to raise money for the missionaries. And every Easter there were the larrikins from the local Cub Scout troop on Bob-a-Job Week, offering to sell their services for 5p. Not surprisingly, that idea came a cropper in the 1990s. Last, but not least, there was the door-to-door salesman, with a battered case of brushes and cleaning gear, or occasionally a set of encyclopedias, his suit slightly crumpled so your Mum felt sorry for him and bought another unnecessary set of dusters, whereupon he disappeared round the corner and into his new Merc.

The door-to-door sales technique got an additional, nasty little twist in the 1980s when the pyramid selling companies got going. Your best friend would suddenly come round and start trying to convince you the thing you most needed in your life was a water-filter jug. As the ads suggested, 'Just say no.' It was the only way to keep friendships alive.

Door-to-door callers have become much more menacing, making aggressive demands for sponsorship for an indeterminate 'fun run' with the money upfront . . . Surely a con. The dusters are still on offer but pitched by a posse of da youth who look like they might ramraid your house if you decline. Oh, and there's the Hallowe'en nightmare, when gangs of sullen hoodies troop round the streets looking for a sugar high.

When my youngest daughter was a baby, I was able to use her as a handy decoy. You answer the door with the baby in your arms, who is preferably crying incessantly, and say, 'Now's not a good time.' When Mr Cold-Caller says, 'Oh, when would be a good time?', you look at your little darling and say to him, 'When she's twenty-three . . .'

Avocado or Old Georgian Lampblack

Interiors

12 September 1976 On a late summer afternoon in Birmingham, photographer Martin Elliott takes a shot of his girlfriend in tennis kit and no knickers – students' walls will never be the same again.

There was an era before TV invented home makeover shows, when interior design was not dictated by a gaggle of foppish consultants cramming an average semi with some leftovers from the Habitat sale. To be successful in 1970s interior design you only had to follow one simple rule: if it moves, cover it with woodchip wallpaper, wall-to-wall carpeting or lashings of Anaglypta.

Like countless other flat-dwellers and home-owners in the 1980s and 1990s, I was destined to spend many hours steaming woodchip off the walls of wherever I moved into – nightmare – and replacing it with thick, chalky, richly coloured paint called Radicchio Red or Lichen Green, only to find that within minutes the kids had scraped it off with their fingers. But I did retain a soft spot for the carpeting, remaining slightly out of step at a time when natural wood floors and stripped boards were in vogue (or in *World of Interiors*, anyway).

Also dating back to the mid-'70s is my penchant for

open fires. This had been a step up from the old two-bar electric heater, with exposed filaments, which would never get past Health and Safety these days: great for lighting fags or toasting crumpets, but if you sat too close for too long your school uniform would start to smoulder gently. And it was a move on from the fake log or coal fires with the rotating orange 'flame'. When we got an open fire in the house, that was the business. Not some modernist excuse for a fire with two pebbles and a Zippo-height flame – this was the real deal, a full-on furnace that could smelt iron.

One of our neighbours added an extra finishing touch – a *Brady Bunch*-style fireplace, a big old brick extravaganza, with an inglenook or two – and I can date my fondness for open brickwork to the moment I first saw that fireplace. But it wasn't easy getting to see it. You had to negotiate a gigantic crystal handle on the front door that was set too close to the wall, so every time you tried to open it your knuckles were scraped red raw.

Neighbours' houses were always good showrooms for new interior design ideas. Some were good: my best chum Paul's family home had a great collection of executive toys, including the classic Newton's cradle and an oddly futuristic Perspex puzzle. Others were weird: the first time I came across a bidet in a posh house I thought, Strange place for a drinking fountain, and was taken aback when told it was for cleaning your arse.

Bathrooms also started to change colour – after decades of nothing but white all hell was let loose. Everyone remembers avocado bathroom suites, but I think ours was more olive, part of the crop of oranges, browns and greens that sprouted up around 1970. Colour co-ordination was paramount: we also had a dinner service that was only brought out on special occasions, a heavy slate-looking set, in which everything was dark brown, even down to the tiny coffee cups and saucers.

Our own and friends' homes were full of pelmets, radiator covers, all-in-one telephone tables and seats (with little phone-number books that popped up when you pressed a letter of the alphabet), coloured plastic strips dangling in the kitchen doorway, serving hatches, nests of tables, lots of stripped pine, and hi-fi units with smoke-effect plastic lids. When we finally got a turntable that let you stack 45 r.p.m. singles and play them one after another, I knew I was living at the cutting edge!

The only place that a kid could establish their own interior world was in their bedroom. OK, before the great duvet revolution you might be forced to sleep on brushed nylon sheets that meant you woke up looking like an electrostatic Worzel Gummidge, but at least you could plaster the walls with any number of BluTak'd posters. Downstairs might be Monet or David Gentleman prints, but upstairs there was an endless choice of music posters (especially the pyramids that came with *The Dark Side of the Moon*, or Bowie as Aladdin Sane) and football squads from *Shoot!* – with the pic taken in the off season after the lads had enjoyed a couple of weeks in Torremolinos, the pitch in perfect condition, and the team's shorts neatly ironed. In a girl's room it was probably Marc Bolan, the Bay City Rollers, Donny Osmond, or that slightly risqué

Annie Leibovitz shot of David Cassidy for *Rolling Stone*, showing him naked with his arms behind his head, with the photo cropped a daring couple of inches below his navel. Later, Duran Duran and Wham! became teenage girls' posters of choice, while Athena helped cover a million students' walls with bare-bottomed tennis girls, James Dean, Marilyn Monroe and that bloke with a baby in his arms.

I ploughed my own furrow through the 1980s – the age of minimalism and bright primary colours – by dodging the futon phase (just too close to the ground), though I did buy a beanbag at some point. I also worked with a press agent whose office was the epitome of the bamboo furniture, cactus and pot plant interior design scheme – 'conservatory chic' I suppose you'd call it. And I have to admit I spent much of the late '80s firmly on the bandwagon of rag-rolling, marbling, stencilling and distressing. In the end I was more distressed than the Welsh dresser (his name's Evan, lovely lad, been working with me for years).

Swap Shop or eBay

Deal or no deal . . .

2 October 1976 BBC1 broadcasts the first *Multi-Coloured Swap Shop*, hosted by Noel Edmonds. The show ran for 146 episodes to March 1982.

When a disgruntled divorcé in Western Australia puts his entire life up for sale on eBay, it makes you wonder just how and why we've ended up in this incessant, all-consuming, globally digital car-boot sale. In the mid-1970s the closest we got to eBay was the bring-and-buy sale at the local vicarage to raise funds for missionary work. And we never made a penny out of it. The same was true of those biscuit tins lined with green crêpe paper and full of tinned fruit salad and frankfurters in brine which we donated to the harvest festival and which were then distributed to the local pensioners (who presumably groaned, 'Not *more* bleedin' peaches').

The truth is probably that we simply didn't own as much crap. The generation who became mums and dads in the '50s and '60s had come through the war, survived rationing and – although happy to embrace the consumer revolution – hadn't the time or the money to amass huge piles of shite.

It all changed when Noel Edmonds, then a Radio One

DJ, popped up behind his desk on *Multi-Coloured Swap Shop*, picked up the little trimphone by his side, and set a generation of kids – today's eBay fanatics – off on a journey of trading up, or down. He's still at it now with *Deal or No Deal*, a show that perfectly captures how to deal with the credit crunch – close your eyes, cross your fingers and fuckin' hope . . .

Cheggers was his alarmingly cheerful accomplice, traipsing around the land with an outside broadcast van in tow. Invariably there would be some poor mug who would end up swapping a bike for a Mastermind board game – for that you should have had Magnus Magnusson thrown in too, so he could sit beside you while you were doing your O levels. Of course, the kid who got the bike was smugly canny, and probably grew up to be the bloke who traded a key ring into a house on eBay thirty years later.

The kids in my street used to set up little stalls from time to time to flog off their old toys and make a few bob to boost their pocket money. My own entrepreneurial activities were rather recherché in comparison. Opposite our house was a stamp dealer, an extraordinary man called Djumic Sandow, an Auschwitz survivor, who handled all the stamps sent in for those annual *Blue Peter* appeals. We'd go in on a Saturday and help him out for some cash in hand, emptying sacks of stamps, alongside his son Robin, sorting them and occasionally coming across odd bits of foreign currency. I must have been fourteen or fifteen when I fished out a note for a million Yemeni rials or Madagascan francs or something like that, niftily pocketed it, and thought, That's it, done, I'm rich now. Alas, my dreams of a leisured life driving Jensen Interceptors and being pleasured by Olivia Newton-John came to a screeching halt when I discovered the note was worth about 5p.

I managed to avoid the car-boot craze, I'm glad to say, and now I'd be far too nervous to go to one. Follow a bunch of cars parking up in a deserted field, pop over to the one with the windows steamed up expecting to buy a tasty burger, and you'll find your neighbours from down the road dogging away to their heart's content, swapping everything – including partners, bodily fluids and an unsavoury collection of STDs!

Post Office Tower or Gherkin

Architecture

25 October 1976 In pouring rain, the Queen opens the much-delayed Denys Lasdun-designed National Theatre on the South Bank.

I have mixed feelings about modern architecture. When they decided to knock down the multi-storey car park on Tyneside that had been a location in *Get Carter*, and a protest group got up in arms, I thought, Come on, it's a car park. But I do also like quite a lot of that brutalist archi-tecture – the National Theatre on the South Bank, for example (despite Prince Charles saying it was a clever way to build a nuclear power station in the heart of London) – just as much as I love Tower Bridge, the Tower of London and the re-gilded Albert Memorial. And the new crop of buildings in the capital like the Gherkin are fabulously imaginative and I'm sure will, along with the London Eye, become just as iconic.

The Post Office Tower was definitely an iconic feature of the London skyline in the late '60s and '70s, part of the legacy of Tony Benn when he was Postmaster General and leading Harold Wilson's crusade to deliver the 'white heat' of technological revolution. I know it's called the BT Tower now, but I can't help thinking of it in old money. It was absolutely in tune with the age, standing high with all the presence of an Apollo mission ready for take-off, bristling with aerials and dishes, but not purely scientific. The perfect touch was that revolving Top of the Tower restaurant, straight out of Tracy Island, a perfect setting for any *Penthouse*-reading international superspy to wine and dine an exotic contact. I can't think why the Bond movies never used the tower as a location. All we got was Noel Edmonds on Christmas Day.

And that reminds me of my other all-time top retro building, Noel's other long-time haunt: the BBC Television Centre in Wood Lane, with its curved façade and walls that could open up to the outside world to let the Sally Army band march straight into the *Blue Peter* studio every Christmas. We knew it was Christmas because all four of the candles on the advent crown made out of metal coat-hangers and tinsel were alight. Now even the BBC Television Centre in west London is under threat. If there's a national treasure that needs to be preserved – other than Christopher Biggins, of course – then that's the one.

Moody cow or emo

Teenage angst

3 November 1976 Release of *Carrie*, the film version of a Stephen King tale, starring Sissy Spacek as the tormented teenager of the title. 'If you've got a taste for terror, take Carrie to the prom.'

When you're a teenager, I guess you always think no one over the age of twenty understands what you're going through, and you *know* your parents have not got a single inkling of the trauma and pain being inflicted on you as you wrestle with your inner angst. Then you reach an age when you realise why no one understood you. They didn't want to go near you, because you didn't wash and you were so bloody miserable. And even if they did, one surly glare from beneath a heavily fringed brow used to cut them off. The surly glare has been replaced by those kids who can't even make eye contact. The only conversation they'll grudgingly give out still goes along the same lines as the teenagers of yore, with only a few minor variations: 'You just don't understand', 'But everybody else has got long hair (for which now read 'nipple ring')', and that all-time favourite, 'I didn't *ask* to be born'.

Misery is part of the rite of passage from little boy to rugged man (and I imagine from little girl to rugged woman, too). In the '70s the answer to a savagely broken heart was simple – lock yourself in your bedroom, cover your spots with a good old dose of Clearasil, crank up some of your brother's Nick Drake or Leonard Cohen albums, and make yourself feel truly, deeply miserable until you were wallowing in the stuff (the misery, not the Clearasil). After a few days' emotional rehab, you were ready to head back into the fray once again. It was back-strengthening stuff, and just what you did. Phil Collins later produced an entire album in *Face Value* to provide a complete soundtrack for the process. I call the whole genre 'music to get divorced to . . .'

A splash to one side here. Spots, acne. Clearasil was the only solution, literally, though one friend of mine is still scarred, not from the acne, but by his mum's helpful suggestion that he use TCP instead, so that his girlfriend's parents always knew when he was in the house by the aromatic trail he left behind him, like the scent of an adolescent skunk. I'm sure there aren't as many kids wandering around with such livid, explosively pustulous faces as we had thirty years ago. They've probably all swiped their mum's credit card and had cosmetic surgery at the first glimpse of a spot. Or maybe they're just washing more than once a week.

Where acne has waned, angst has waxed. Like nut allergies and asthma – both virtually unheard of when I was at school – self-harm and loathing seem to be on an alarmingly upward track. A sensitive teenage girl in the 1970s suffering from mood swings? 'Snap out of it, you moody cow' would have been the empathetic response. Now, she can join the cult of emo. I don't know much about emo, just observe it from the outside, but I can spot the tell-tale signs – floppy fringes, drainpipe jeans, lashings of mascara, a bit like Johnny Ramone. Perhaps being part of a cult helps when you're at that point in your life when you're trying to work out what the hell it's all about.

I might not have to wait too long to experience the teenage years again. They say kids are growing up faster now, and I have conclusive proof that it's true. My daughter, aged six, declared to me only the other day that school was 'getting in the way of the rest of my life, Dad'.

Parky or Paxman

Interview technique

27 November 1976 One of the most famous moments in the history of Michael Parkinson's chat show, when he goes mano-a-mano and beak-to-beak with Rod Hull's Emu.

Saturday evening on BBC1, just before *Match of the Day*, was Parkinson time. Laurie Holloway at the piano leading the band in a cracking theme tune, full of snap and sophistication, Parky tiptapping down the staircase as fleet-footed as Fred Astaire, and a top-flight, A-list trio of guests. Although he might have lost a little snap at the tail-end of his career, Michael Parkinson in his prime was an astute celebrity interviewer, who – like Jeremy Paxman and all the best interviewers – had been a proper journalist, trained on a gritty local newspaper, then the *Manchester Guardian*, and his talents honed by Granada TV (the station named after a holiday trip to southern Spain by co-founder Cecil Bernstein).

Parky always attracted big, big names. Before inundation by the digital press pack, and with the limited number of channels, an interview with Parky was often the only chance a British audience had to see the great Hollywood or Broadway stars live, a Liza Minnelli or a Robert Redford, alongside the best of British talent – Peter Cook, perhaps, or Richard Burton, who made one appearance fresh out of rehab and thought the BBC catering staff in their white coats had come to take him away . . .

Parkinson also acted as an informal talent show, launching Peter Kay, who was a warm-up for the programmes, as well as springboarding Billy Connolly from cultish folk musician with a few gags into national figure, mainly due to one joke (the one about the bum and the bicycle). Parky was genuinely interested in his guests, or clever enough to seem interested, but he was no pushover. Don't forget that when he was chosen to fill the shoes of the departed Roy Plomley on *Desert Island Discs*, he lasted only a couple of years before his 'aggressive' questioning led him to be ousted in favour of Sue Lawley.

Parkinson's shadow loomed over all his competitors and successors, and I don't think any of them quite lived up to his high standards, no matter how talented or amusing they were. Russell Harty goaded Grace Jones into whacking him, while Clive Anderson's dry questions caused the Bee Gees to flounce out. In later years people complained that Parky was too easy on guests (Meg Ryan would probably disagree), but he was the master of drawing out a reluctant celebrity until they said something interesting or revealing. And when he *did* have a fight with a guest, at least he picked on someone bigger than himself – notably the fearsomely articulate Muhammad Ali and the even more terrifying (if less articulate) Emu.

After time off on *Give Us a Clue* and other undemanding fare, Parkinson returned to a prime-time TV world that had changed out of all recognition. In the wake of programmes like Terry Christian's *The Word* and Chris Evans' *TFI Friday*, and for an audience used to Graham Norton or Mrs Merton asking questions that Parky would never dare or deign to ask, the guru of chat shows seemed a little off the pace, and short of the speed of riposte that Jonathan Ross has down to a T.

Parkinson's great skill as an interviewer was listening, and if I have a criticism of the recent breed of hard news-driven interviewers – whether it's Paxo or the *Today* crew – it's that they never listen, just interrupt. Be interesting to see *them* go a few rounds with the great Ali.

Strewth or *!@*!*

Swearing

1 December 1976 The Sex Pistols cause outrage by swearing at presenter Bill Grundy on the Thames Television programme, *Today*.

The wonderful thing about swearing, as Tigger might have sung if A.A. Milne had decided to call him Frigger, is that it's timeless. The best English swear words are resolutely Anglo-Saxon and always will be. They're too good to replace. But what has changed since I first heard a four-letter word is *where* I now hear them. Part of the illicit joy of the F-word – the best of the bunch – was using it out of earshot of adults whose strongest curse (in their kids' hearing, at least) was 'botheration' when they hammered a nail into their thumb. Other quaintly tame adult oaths included 'Gordon Bennett', 'ruddy', 'crikey Moses', 'flipping Nora' and 'strewth' (or 'strewth alive' if they were *really* angry).

That's why the Sex Pistols saying 'fuck' on prime-time television in 1976 caused such an outrage. I remember watching their famous interview with Bill Grundy when Steve Jones called the veteran presenter a 'dirty fucker'. It was shocking to hear it, let alone on early evening TV. Across the nation a million housewives must have turned from the washing-up bowl, their arms swathed in mild green Fairy Liquid bubbles, as their little treasures ran into the kitchen, expecting them to ask how they managed to keep their hands so soft, only to be told, 'Mum, the Sex Pistols said "fuck" on telly.'

Like everything that gets overused, swearing has lost its impact. What irks me most are the double standards on TV. Past the watershed – an arbitrary line in the sand, since most stroppy kids stay up way past their 'bedtime' – *nothing* is out of line, but before then there's the farce of soaps like *EastEnders* where not a single oath passes even the hardest git's lips while the Queen Vic is torched or mass murder is committed between the market stalls.

The correct use of the swear word should always be when you least expect it. From one of the rag mags that students hawked before the PC police gutted their contents, there was a joke that featured that perennial schoolboy pain in the arse, little Johnny. His swearing had got so out of control that Miss Jones, his teacher, was at her wits' end. One day, she thought she'd found the solution. 'Good morning, class,' she said brightly. 'Today I want you to tell me what you did last night, and I want you to use the word "nice" twice.' That should stop Johnny from swearing, she reckoned. 'Who's first?' At the back of the class, Johnny had his hand up like a shot, but she chose Annabel at the front. 'Well, miss, when I got back home after school, my mum had bought me a nice brand-new dress, and I said, "Thanks, Mum, that's really nice."' 'Excellent, excellent, Annabel, that's very good. Who's next?' From the back of the class, Johnny pleaded, 'Me, me, miss.' Again he was ignored, and Miss Jones pointed to Kevin. 'Yes, miss, I did my homework and then had a nice game of Monopoly with my brother, and then we had a really nice supper of baked beans on toast.' 'Good work, Kevin.' Eventually, Miss Jones had worked round the whole class, and everyone had had a go except Johnny, who was still lying across his desk with his hand up. 'OK, Johnny, why don't you tell us your story, and don't forget to use the word "nice" twice,' she said. 'Thank you, miss. Well, last night I had my dinner and I was watching TV when our old cat, Boots, who hasn't been feeling very well, was sick right under the coffee table. Just then, my dad got back in from work. He saw where Boots had been sick and said, "Oh, that's nice, that's really *fucking* nice."'

ABBA: The Movie or Mamma Mia!: The Movie

Guilty pleasures

3 March 1977 Benny, Björn, Anni-Frid and Agnetha play their first concert at the Sydney Showgrounds, the opening date on their triumphant tour of Australia, which provided the bulk of the footage for *ABBA: The Movie*.

Guilty secrets pop out at the least likely moments. Late 1977, at school, I was walking across the playground when I was approached by a bloke I thought of as quite a hard geezer. I wasn't sure why he wanted to talk to me, and was thinking up a couple of escape plans, when he totally took me aback by saying, 'You seen *ABBA: The Movie*?' (silence) 'You should. It's pretty good. I really like that song "Eagle".' You could've knocked me down with the prover-bial friggin' feather. This totally unexpected secret confession immediately validated my own fondness for ABBA – and I'd seen the movie as well, and enjoyed its rockumentary vibe, because I was too young to go and see Led Zep in *The Song Remains the Same*.

It was OK to be a Slade fan, even if they were quite cheesy, because the drummer looked hard, Dave Hill's haircut looked mad, and they couldn't spell, so that made them acceptable. David Cassidy was a touch girly. The

---

Osmonds were probably the wrong side of admissible, even though 'Crazy Horses' was their best song. But Marie and Little Jimmy, or the Carpenters, no way: Karen Carpenter dressed like your mum in a frock made out of flock wallpaper. So even if the singles sounded good, you'd deny any knowledge.

I don't know what the equivalent would be today. Maybe bumping into Ray Winstone and him saying, 'You seen *Mamma Mia: The Movie*?' (silence) 'You should. You'll love it.' Or owning up to watching every episode of *Celebrity* . . . fuckwits poncing round on an island. And I'm not owning up to it, by the way. I did recently out myself as a Genesis fan in an interview, and promptly found myself asked by the band to MC the premiere of their tour documentary *Come Rain or Shine*. I imagine nobody else had dared 'fess up, though I was delighted that Al Murray (the Pub Landlord) was prepared to come along and lend his support, so I didn't feel completely alone. It was like being at a meeting of GA (Genesis Anonymous). 'Hi, my name's Phil and I like *The Lamb Lies Down on Broadway*.'

Johnny Rotten or John Lydon

Never mind the bollocks

10 March 1977 The Sex Pistols sign to A&M Records outside Buckingham Palace. The deal was scrapped six days later and the Pistols signed with Virgin instead to release 'God Save the Queen' in time for the Silver Jubilee celebrations.

Punk very nearly passed me by. A swift scan of my CDs (extremely Luddite, I agree – I'm still working on my iTunes playlists as I write, honestly) will reveal what you might think a rather high percentage of Pink Floyd, Genesis (see above) and Focus. You don't remember Focus? Dutch band, guitarist with the physique of a Rotterdam stevedore, keyboard player with a ridiculously high falsetto voice – marvellous. I tried to get 'Sylvia', their only chart success, on to the soundtrack for *Life on Mars* – great for a car-chase – but we were asked for too much money. Even Paul McCartney, who must have been weighing up the likely cost of his divorce with Heather, let us use 'Live and Let Die'.

So you have an idea of my tastes, all of which, on the endlessly churning cycle of popular music, will soon be cutting edge again – OK, maybe not Focus. But I was not immune to punk. I liked the Pistols. And the Clash's 'London Calling'.

Punk was a great catalyst – we're still seeing the after-shock in fashion and design, but less so in music. The punks who signed with major labels, the Pistols included, ended up playing the Tin Pan Alley game, and you knew they'd sold out when Kid Jensen or DLT introduced the Damned on *Top of the Pops*.

But the wonderful thing is that the old punks have become the very establishment they spat at. Mick Jones may have been responsible for 'London Calling' and pro-duced the Libertines, but there he was supping Evian at Wimbledon '08 and celebrating his birthday with a lovely pink cake.

And Johnny Rotten is now John Lydon esquire. He's still jaunty, still has plenty of acerbic vim left – 'I'm fat, I'm fifty and I'm *back*,' he told an audience recently. But the anarchist who was called 'the biggest threat to our youth since Hitler' has since had his teeth redone for ten grand, the midriff shows a bit of a spare tyre and he's been mar-ried to the same woman for decades. Good for him, but not exactly what you'd expect from a self-proclaimed Antichrist. His appearance on *I'm a Celebrity* . . . put him in severe danger of becoming a national treasure, up there with Stephen Fry, Judi Dench or HRH herself. And I heard that he now sports a pair of bifocals. Snappy and steel-rimmed, sure, but still bifocals. That's reassuring for any of us who are heading for an age where it's going to be less 'sex and drugs and rock'n'roll', more 'Sussex, rugs and Anusol'.

Roger Moore or Daniel Craig

James Bond

7 July 1977 World premiere at the Odeon Leicester Square of *The Spy Who Loved Me*, the opening sequence featuring the classic Union Jack skydiving stunt performed by Rick Sylvester at Mount Asgard on Baffin Island in Canada.

It's a perennial poser. Who's been the best James Bond: Connery, Lazenby, Moore, Dalton, Brosnan or Craig (and you could throw David Niven into that mix for his appearance in the first *Casino Royale*)? The question is ultimately unanswerable, which is why we'll be able to chew over the possibilities for decades – and many more Bonds – to come.

Perhaps the reality is that the Bond you like best is the one you grew up with, the one who starred in the first Bond movies you watched. Roger Moore was the Bond who dominated the 1970s and 1980s, from *Live and Let Die* in 1973 (my first-ever Bond movie) to *A View to a Kill* a dozen years later, and one of the best Bonds in the franchise was *The Spy Who Loved Me*, which I saw when we were on holiday in north Wales in a tiny cinema on Anglesey.

Roger was the Cary Grant of Bonds, with a natural gift for light comedy. One great Bond moment that springs to mind is in *Moonraker*. After the traditional scrap with the evil henchman on top of a cable car in Rio, and with Jaws dispatched to the valley floor, Roger is left dangling in space. Lois Chiles as Holly Goodhead looks over and calls out: 'James, just hang on!' One Moore eyebrow goes up, two beats, then: 'The thought had occurred to me.' Cracking. Only Rog could have delivered that line so perfectly. He wasn't the Bond that Ian Fleming wrote, but he was spot on in the version of the character that he created.

Each of the other Bonds has had their particular strengths, some more than others – and don't forget that one of the first Bonds was none other than Bob 'Blockbusters' Holness (in a mid-'50s South African radio version of *Moonraker*); little factoid there. I saw Daniel Craig in *Casino Royale*. Great casting, the right Bond for the twenty-first century.

Bond girls are far harder to choose between because they're all gorgeous, but let's have a go. From the Roger Moore era, Jane Seymour as Solitaire, Britt Ekland as Miss Mary Goodnight, Barbara Bach as Anya Amasova – stunning, the lot of them – and more recently Sophie Marceau in *The World Is Not Enough*.

Bond themes? Again, it's Rog and *The Spy Who Loved Me*, with 'Nobody Does It Better'. Carly Simon, Marvin Hamlisch, Carole Bayer Sager – great song and plenty of Broadway pedigree.

And the best stunt is universally accepted as the opening sequence of the same movie, with Rick Sylvester launching himself into the void to unfurl the Union Jack as the music kicks in. On Anglesey, and in cinemas up and down the country, audiences broke into spontaneous applause. I heard that the film unit had seven cameras set up to cover all the angles and six of them jammed, scaring the living shit out of the director. But one kept running and got the money shot. As 007 told M, the Russian general and the Minister of Defence as they watched a screen showing him *in flagrante* with 'Triple X', he's been 'keeping the British end up' for over forty years.

Benidorm or Dubai

Overseas holidays

1 September 1977 Freddie Laker inaugurates Skytrain, the first low-cost airline, with flights from London Gatwick to New York. Rival airlines ganged up on him, and by 1982 Skytrain had gone bust.

One of the great shifts in the 1970s was the move to overseas holidays and the beginning of the demise of the traditional British seaside summer break (although the latter is now experiencing a revival, by all accounts, courtesy of the old credit crunch).

The first package holidays from companies like Thomas Cook came into vogue in the '70s, fuelled by the spirit of wanderlust conveyed by Cliff Michelmore and Judith Chalmers on *Holiday* and *Wish You Were Here* on dark evenings at the start of each new year. These were the days when the basic *'España por favor'* package was a whizz down to the Costa Blanca, Brava or del Sol and back, to resorts like Benidorm, Tossa de Mar and Torremolinos where families could embrace the local culture with menus that offered an all-purpose Euro-lunch of 'bifteck mit chips'. The same formula could then easily be applied worldwide, eventually rippling out to the Canary Islands, the Maldives, the Seychelles, the Caribbean or Dubai. And let's face it, a couple of weeks lying in guaranteed sun was a great selling point, compared to the prospect of a wet fortnight in Skegness (and please, good folk of Skeggie, I could have picked any resort in Britain, I'm not having a go at you personally – in fact, I'm looking forward to my book signing on the seafront).

Now, my family never went on a package holiday. No, we were far too middle class for that. Our overseas adventures were all about driving holidays in France. Trundling on to the ferry at Dover, or in a kind of futuristic, *Tomorrow's World* version – the hovercraft – to invade the Pas-de-Calais and head south. We were just as much sun-seekers as the 18–30 crowd, but we were able to dress it up as a cultural excursion by drinking lots of *vin de pays*, visiting a château or two and experimenting with quiche lorraine and crème brûlée.

These holidays meant getting up at four in the morning to load the car up, and triple-check that we'd a) turned off the gas, b) cancelled the milk and c) cancelled the papers, because it was common knowledge that if you failed to do any one of a), b) or c) the house would be burgled immediately or squatters would take up residence for the duration. Now at least you don't need to worry about any of that, because you can set off on holiday absolutely secure in the knowledge that the newsagent's son will GoogleEarth your house to see if you've got a decent swimming pool and immediately send out an invite on Facebook for half of Hampshire to come and trash your garden. No problem.

The penultimate element of the preparations was

applying the headlight converters, although that took *all* the fun out of blinding Pernod-crazed French drivers coming the other way after sundown. And finally I would be allowed to apply the finishing touch to the car, the adhesive GB plate, freshly supplied by the ferry company. The continent beckoned. An endless summer of continental breakfasts, baguettes, bowls of hot chocolate, pétanque, Tintin books and espadrilles – then all exotically Gallic, now all available at Asda.

Hamster or Nintendog

Pets

14 September 1977 Petra, the *Blue Peter* dog, dies. She is not buried, as myth would later have it, in Percy Thrower's *Blue Peter* Garden, but a bust of her is unveiled there two years later.

I'm not good with pets. At junior school we used to take it in turns to take home Jeffrey the hamster. When my turn came, I had to lug this bloody big cage all the way back to our house. We had no idea what we were doing. My mum suggested a bowl of water. We waited for a while, then thought it might be a good idea to let Jeffrey outside in the garden for a walk. Off he toddled, and vanished. We never saw him again, I kid you not. We searched everywhere, but Jeffrey had taken his chance for freedom. My mum wrote a note to my teacher on best blue Basildon Bond – 'Terribly sorry, we've lost the hamster. We'll pay for a new one' – and made me lug the empty cage back to school with the letter propped up on the straw like a message from the crib. Highly embarrassing, of course, but amazingly the school made no fuss. Today the RSPCA would be round like a shot: 'OK, up against the wall, sonny, what have you done with the hamster? What were the rodent's last-known movements?'

None the less, and perhaps unwisely, we then got a

rabbit, which we called Hopalong. If I play that game where you add the name of your first pet to your own middle name to create your porn-star persona, I'd be Hopalong Haywood. But he did a runner too. If my kids ask me now, 'Can we have a pet, please, Dad?' I can't quite face it. 'Sorry, girls, I've got form.'

Our lack of pet-keeping skills was puzzling. Pets – certainly if you watched *Blue Peter*, because the cooler *Magpie* on the other side naturally didn't have them – seemed quite undemanding things: docile dogs, serene Siamese or tabbie cats, a tortoise that took a nap in the autumn and didn't wake up till Easter. Maybe I should have had a tortoise.

Pearl & Dean or multiscreen

Cinemas

27 December 1977 Star Wars finally reaches British cinemas, seven months after its US release: the film will be the highest-grossing movie to date.

There was a time when if you wanted to see a movie you had to go to the cinema. How quaint that seems. And when the film had left town, that was it. Until, years later, it might be shown on TV. How weird is that?

The cinema experience was a special one. And wonderfully, in some ways, it hasn't changed too much. As soon as I enter the portals of an Odeon or a Vue, I still feel that insane physical craving to eat popcorn – swilled down with a large bucket of Coke – that I never feel at any other time or in any other place. I thought video, and later DVDs and downloads, might kill not just the radio star but the film star. Yet, against the odds, cinema is still going strong. OK, there aren't many of the classic old cinemas left – those fantastical buildings called the Alhambra or the Majestic – and we watch the new releases in soulless multiplexes where Screen 7 is smaller than the next-door neighbour's plasma, but the movie business has stuck with it, and film premieres, BAFTAs and Oscars continue to be headline-makers. And there is still the fascination with movies, their impact and their scale that once upon a time powered not just Chris Kelly's *Clapperboard*, but also *Screen Test*, hosted by Michael Rodd (who I always got mixed up with John Craven – their hairstyles seemed interchangeable, or maybe they shared the same BBC wig).

Because downloading a movie on to your iPhone may be handy but it's just not the same experience as looking at a huge great screen. Widescreen is king. Those great movies in the tradition of *The Battle of Britain* and *Where Eagles Dare* (my first cinemagoing experience in the late '60s) had to be viewed in larger-than-life Todd-AO widescreen format, with Kia-Ora and a half-time ice-cream – from the usherette's tray – between the B-movie and the main feature.

And who doesn't miss those semi-pro local ads that sat alongside the Pearl & Dean sequence, with the same toffee-nosed geezer voicing all of them? 'For the authentic taste of the Indian subcontinent, visit the Taj Mahal, at 241 on Kenton High Street.' Next ad, same voice: 'For all your motoring requirements, visit Kenton Motors, at 243 on Kenton High Street.'

Jordan the punk or Jordan the pink

Jordans

23 February 1978 Derek Jarman's *Jubilee*, a nihilistic punk counterblast to the previous year's Silver Jubilee celebrations, premieres, with Toyah Willcox as Mad and Jordan as Amyl Nitrite.

There are two wonderful Jordans. One was the punk icon, born Pamela Rooke in Seaford, Sussex – what a wonderful birthplace for a punk icon! She was a shop assistant at the Sex boutique on the King's Road, an essential component of the Malcolm McLaren/Sex Pistols entourage with her trademark platinum-blond spikes and heavy mascara, and for Vivienne Westwood became a cross between a mobile clothes horse and a guinea pig (those bloody genetic experiments). Then, as Amyl Nitrite in Derek Jarman's film *Jubilee*, she was a quite extraordinary Britannia. Punk, said Jordan, really died once the Pistols split up. 'It couldn't have gone on – it was like an orgasm . . . A few seconds, then *pffft*.'

And the other wonderful Jordan is a sacred river without which we would never have had a decent English rugby anthem!

DLT or Moylesy

DJs

2 May 1978 Dave Lee Travis, the 'Hairy Monster', takes over Radio One's *Breakfast Show* from Noel Edmonds: DLT dubs himself the 'Hairy Cornflake'.

Thursday evening after dinner, and *Top of the Pops* was a chance to see the Radio One DJs' smiling mugs squeezed between a bevy of manically grinning fans bussed in for the evening. The job wasn't particularly demanding, a simple bit of autocue for a ten-second link, giving the name of the group and the single they were about to mime to on stage. Even so, John Peel managed to slide in the odd caustic remark whenever he was persuaded on to the show: really he was a late-night owl, and far too credible to introduce the Brotherhood of Man. But even those of us who listened to Peel or Little Nicky Horne on Capital Radio, or watched the TV equivalent, *The Old Grey Whistle Test*, still happily tuned in to *TOTP*, because we bought singles and wanted to know what or what not to buy. It was all very democratic: massive megastars would be on next to bizarre novelty acts and, before the invention of pop videos, any group who couldn't make it to appear live could rest assured that Pan's People would do their very best to interpret the lyrics as literally as possible.

Many of the DJs who made regular appearances had been the pioneers of pirate radio and then Radio One: Tony Blackburn, the first voice on the new station when it launched in September 1967, Ed 'Stewpot' Stewart, Kenny Everett, in yellow badge-laden dungarees, and the aviator specs of Simon Bates, later joined by Peter Powell ('leave it out, mate') and the hirsute one, the Hairy Monster himself, DLT. I had a particular fondness for the Emperor Rosko, primarily because of that definite article. Not just Emperor Rosko, but *the* Emperor Rosko. *The Chart Show*, at a time when there was only the one singles chart, was an essential Sunday afternoon and early evening event, leading up to the Number One just before 7 p.m., and absolutely had to be taped if you couldn't listen to it in real time.

After their stints on Radio One, the survivors shuffled over to Radio Two – the moment when the original DJs officially became square was when Mike Read barred Frankie Goes To Hollywood's 'Relax' – and when they became even more superannuated they could be found accepting the radio equivalent of the Chiltern Hundreds (that will be Chiltern 100 FM, broadcasting live from downtown Princes Risborough), hosting golden-oldie shows on Melody FM. It's good to see and hear that their successors, especially on the *Breakfast Show*, have kept the flag flying, with Chris Moyles stirring in some controversy, to keep Radio One alive when there are so many other music stations to choose from. I came across one the other week which announced it was broadcasting music 'to south-west London'. Why?

I tried my hand once as a DJ, on hospital radio, a

training ground for future DLTs when there were no media studies courses. On our first day we were issued with a detailed list of songs that we were advised not to play as they might upset the patients. The list opened with 'I Left My Heart in San Francisco' and was rounded off by 'Staying Alive', 'The Final Countdown' and 'Knocking on Heaven's Door'.

Swinging or dogging

Love thy neighbour

10 June 1978 After three years of nudge-nudge wink-wink allusions to wife-swapping, Felicity Kendal, Penelope Keith and co. wrap up *The Good Life* with a one-off live show in front of the Queen and Prince Philip.

The word out on the streets – or the gravel drives – was that if any of the neighbours had planted pampas grass in their front garden, that meant they were swingers. I don't think I really knew what 'swinging' meant, but its image was very middle class, a social circle populated by couples like Jerry and Margo Leadbetter off *The Good Life* inviting you in for a glass of sherry and a shag in a posh house with a brass plaque by the front door saying, 'Don't ring if you don't swing.'

At least there was a thin veneer of civilised behaviour about it all, unlike the delightfully named activity of dogging – nothing to do with Crufts, though wouldn't it be fun to find Peter Purves popping up from the back seat of your motor and proffering the immortal line, 'What a glorious bitch.'? If I was going to be polyamorous, I'd have been a swinger. However, I didn't have any car keys at the time, and I was never sure throwing a student bus pass in the bowl would find many takers.

The Good Old Days or Life on Mars

Nostalgia

21 July 1978 The very last broadcast of the BBC's *Black and White Minstrel Show*. Three years earlier Lenny Henry had been the first black guest to appear on it.

Nostalgia, they say, ain't what it used to be. The TV shows from the '70s that traded in blatant nostalgia harked back to the early part of the century. *The Good Old Days* was a blast from the past for our grandparents' generation, an excuse for their peers to get togged up in Edwardian clothes, the gents in boaters and stripy waistcoats, their lady friends in feather boas and tight bodices, and cram into an old theatre for a night of music-hall fun. The proceedings were hosted by Leonard Sachs, whose trademark introductions were elaborately florid, full of oracular orotundity and Brobdingnagian bravura (cue audience going 'ooooh'). Music-hall turns must have been hard to find, though, because every time Leonard worked himself up into another torrent of verbal verisimilitude (ooooh) and announced the next act of positively prodigious pulchritude (oooooh), it was always, *always*, Danny La Rue and a squad of can-can girls.

Another throwback to the early twentieth century was *The Black and White Minstrel Show*, still going strong well into the late '70s, and on prime-time Saturday evenings. Grown men blacking up to sing 'Ol' Man River', with the same can-can team from *The Good Old Days* given a quick lick of greasepaint and transformed into whorehouse hoofers. What an odd programme. No commissioning editor would dream of going near it now, but I don't remember anyone batting an eyelid at the time, though I'm sure anybody watching it who had slave roots would have disagreed.

Around the same time sitcom writers started mining the comic potential of their own youths. The thirty-year rule came into force – the moment when out-of-date memories become cherished nostalgia, and just before they cause neuralgia. David Croft and Jimmy Perry produced *Dad's Army*, and the team's wartime gags continued with *It Ain't Half Hot, Mum* before they moved on to the 1950s and provided *Hi-de-Hi* for a 1980s audience, a decade when the '50s were all the rage: Nick Kamen in the Levi's laundrette ad, Madonna singing 'True Blue', *Back to the Future*. And so it goes on. Come the 2000s and the time was ripe for *Life on Mars*.

One of the strange things about making a 1970s nostalgia show in the 2000s is that it is incredibly hard to find authentic locations because so much of the architecture from that period has been swept away by the developers' JCBs. When everything was shot in studios that wouldn't have been an issue, but now, in the quest for realism, as many scenes as possible are shot on location. Even a couple of the places in Manchester that were used in the first series of *Life on Mars* had disappeared by the time it came to shoot series two.

Amazingly, it's easier to film older period dramas. For a series like *Cranford*, there are still plenty of little places in the Cotswolds, where the National Trust keeps the modern protuberances under control, and a few bags of horse shite are very effective at covering the double-yellow lines on the high street. Whereas in any modern setting, the first job for the props team is to camouflage the satellite dishes. Forget I even said that – I wouldn't want to ruin the illusion.

David Nixon or David Blaine

Now that's magic

1 December 1978 David Nixon dies at the age of fifty-eight from lung cancer – he had been a heavy smoker. The twinkly Anita Harris was his most famous assistant.

Magic, '70s style – David Nixon, genial, charming, twinkly, balding. The epitome of avuncular. A children's entertainer with tricks. Just like your grandad, but without the Werther's Originals. His magic set for Christmas was a must, with mini-wand, a couple of coin tricks and a pack of fixed playing cards.

Magic, '80s style – Paul Daniels, genial, twinkly, balding.

Magic, '90s style – David Copperfield. Blimey, Dickens in Las Vegas. Big production numbers, making the Great Wall of China Wall disappear.

Magic, noughties style – David Blaine. What's with this David thing, by the way? Do all magicians have to be called David (Mr Daniels excluded) or something? Anyway, David Blaine, the David Brent of magic – embarrassing. Living in a box for days on end, shivering in a block of ice, holding your breath for six months or whatever – that's not magic, that's showing off, like the kid at school who'd shove nettles up his nose for a dare; the same one who could always be relied on, if lessons were dragging, to produce a fart sound by putting his hand into his armpit.

Short back and sides or back, sack and crack

Male grooming

7 December 1978 The *Wall Street Journal* announces that Victor Kiam has acquired Remington, the event that prompted his famous TV sales pitch for the Remington shaver: 'I liked it so much, I bought the company!'

The children of the children of the '70s came up with a brilliant way of upsetting their parents. They couldn't freak them out with sex or drugs or rock'n'roll, because all of that had already been done. The horses had been well and truly frightened. It seemed as though all the teenage rebellion that could ever happen had happened. So how could these new teenagers strike fear into those former rebels who were now better known as Mum and Dad? Through body adornment and excessive grooming, that's how. It was a master stroke, something the Woodstock generation had completely overlooked. For the long hair and Afghan coat brigade, extreme body adornment had only meant the terrible threat of being forced to undergo short back and sides.

Tribal and full-body tattoos. Crikey. Rings and studs by the dozen through every available flap and orifice. Ouch. Ramming a Prince Albert through your crown jewels.

Yuuugh. And finally, removing every last hair from the surface of your skin, nether regions included. I'll stop now – I'm waxing lyrical and it bloody hurts

Cloughie or Capello

Football management

9 February 1979 Brian Clough signs Trevor Francis for Nottingham Forest, making the striker the first million-pound footballer. However, Clough disputes this, saying the fee was only £999,999.

I based some of Gene Hunt on football managers of the '70s, particularly Brian Clough. Cloughie was part of the national fabric, his voice and observations always dry and forthright. When he was awarded the OBE, he said it stood for Old Big 'Ead. You've got to love somebody like that.

I came across a clip of Cloughie when I was doing some research for the character. (Yes, that's 'research'. You probably thought it was just a matter of picking up a camel-hair coat from the costume department, organising a Watneys Party Seven tasting and then winging it.) I came across a *Match of the Day* DVD with some footage of the great man being interviewed. 'Mr Clough, what happens if one of your players disagrees with you?' 'Well, they come to see me, we talk about it for twenty minutes, they realise I was right all along, we move on.' That was the attitude for Gene Hunt I was looking for.

Cloughie was not alone. The other First Division

managers were a gallery of majestic characters. Bill Shankly – everyone knows the 'more important than life and death' quote, but I heard a story that the wife of one of the Liverpool players was about to give birth, and half an hour before kick-off he got a call that she had gone into labour. He was about to get his coat and go when Shankly stopped him. 'Don't worry, son, we'll send the sub on for you – does he know the way to the hospital?'

Malcolm Allison – fedora, sheepskin and cigar. Tommy Docherty – great one-liners: 'I've always said there's a place for the press, but they haven't dug it yet', 'Elton John decided he wanted to rename Watford and call it Queen of the South.' Ron Atkinson at West Brom – the first top-flight side to field three black guys in the team on a regular basis – which made it ironic that an unguarded racist remark years later led to his public disgrace. All were larger than life, flamboyant personalities, which is why we still love a Jose Mourinho whenever he crops up.

The England coaches were English, and it does sadden me that they are no longer. Alf Ramsey was an interesting man, like a headmaster – 'Pay attention at the back, Stiles' – and he was followed by a series of English appointees. Now, granted, we didn't win a thing after Alf's time in charge, and I can't blame the sweet FA for looking elsewhere, especially when the last try with the old brolly wally proved just as fruitless. Fabio Capello at least looks like he has some of the Ramsey disciplinarian about him, possibly more so. Instead of viewing videos of the opponents, he probably makes the team watch *The Godfather*. Missed an open goal? Just watch out for the horse's head next to your WAG's thong. Roll on 2010.

Hot Wheels or Grand Theft Auto IV

Toys for boys

3 March 1979 'General Lee', the full-sized version of the Hot Wheels 1969 Dodge Charger, features in the first BBC showing of *The Dukes of Hazzard*, starring alongside Luke, Bo, Boss Hogg and Daisy Duke's cut-off denim shorts.

I was a boy. I had toys. Our local toy shop was Hurley's Library, a real adventure trip each time, the thrill of going into a Mecca of toys. But, and it's a sad admission, I never had Scalextric. Not the Formula One set or the Monte Carlo rally set with its twisty mountain routes. Just Hot Wheels at friends' houses, if I was lucky. Meccano? Nope, never had that either, too damn complicated. That was stuff for the kids who wanted to be mechanical engineers, or who insisted on sitting in the front row for the Royal Institution Christmas Lectures, in the hope that they'd be picked out to help with an experiment or demonstration; and for the rest of us simply a reminder that as soon as the lectures began Christmas was now officially over, and that when they finished we'd be back to school before you could say 'Eric Laithwaite and his linear induction motor.'

I never had a model railway, no Hornby double-O, no little mailbag van, no *Flying Scotsman*. Has it damaged me? I don't know.

But, deprived as I was of these crucial boys' toys, I still had my Action Man. Although he was eventually available in 2 Para and SAS uniforms, we all knew he was really an American dude (known over there as GI Joe). Pedigree Toys produced a patriotic British equivalent, Tommy Gunn, for a few years, but he proved no match for the US version, who came with a macho scar and 'gripping hands'. Maybe when Action Man was off duty he got it on with Barbie. I don't know, but he could definitely have kicked the crap out of Ken.

One of my earliest TV roles was in an episode of *Soldier Soldier*. For part of the filming we had to go and train with the paratroopers in Aldershot. Before we went down there, I asked my chum Nick, who'd been in the army, what sort of bloke joined the paras. 'Do you remember that kid at school who used to stand in the corner of the playground banging his head against the wall? Well, that's the sort of bloke who joins the paras.' They were hard, those boys, seriously hard. And the training was unrelenting, drilled under the command of a sergeant who was the spitting image of Action Man, right down to the scar on his cheek.

More boys' toys, Airfix kits, involved a whole protocol of behaviour. Using Spitfires, Hurricanes and Messerschmitts, I re-enacted the Battle of Britain in downtown Harrow Weald. I went so far as creating clouds out of cotton wool to dangle from my bedroom ceiling, although I just stopped short of painting it blue. The planes were painted with tiny tins of Humbrol paint, a remarkable range of camouflage greens, duck-egg blue for the under-fuselage, masking tape to protect the non-paint areas, then transfers – RAF roundels, Luftwaffe swastikas – to be soaked off in luke-warm water. My personal phobia was smudging the Airfix glue – much thicker than the rival Revell version – on to the plastic of the windscreen. Perfectionist that I am, if that windscreen got marked, I'd have to start all over again. I could spend an entire half-term holiday working on one kit. Airfix also produced packs of miniature soldiers, and *High Chaparral* cowboys, figurines we could play war games with, pontoon bridges stretched across the carpet. I once overstepped my competence by buying a Kawasaki motor-bike kit, which was almost as difficult as building the real thing.

Other toy memories were Corgi and Dinky cars: *Captain Scarlet* cars, the classic Bond Aston Martin DB5, the lunar module. If I was twelve now I'd be stuck in front of my Grand Theft Auto and miss the fun of Matchbox cars flying across the room on Hot Wheels tracks. And those bits and bobs at the bottom of the Rice Krispies box.

One last thought. Airfix's Lancaster bomber had a little guy in the rear gunner's position, and we used to emulate him by swivelling in a tree house with an air gun. It's probably no longer legal even to own an air gun, but back then we sprayed pellets asunder with liberal abandon like Bernie the Bolt and *The Golden Shot* team running amok. I ask you, which is better: shooting pellets from an air rifle, or shooting assorted pimps and dealers on screen in Grand Theft Auto? The technology's different, but I guess boys will be boys.

The Golden Bear or Tiger

Golf

3 May 1979 Denis Thatcher instantly becomes the nation's most famous amateur golfer after his wife Margaret wins the 1979 General Election.

Golf clubhouses and the committee rooms inside them have often displayed a resistance to change equalled only by the more hardline elements of the Vatican. Rule changes were fought over with as much ferocity as a yard of mud at Ypres. The insistence on the exclusion of women from their inner sanctums – though you're always welcome to drop by for a little drink, my dear – is only slowly being eroded. The golf club is a stout final redoubt of male chauvinism. Colonel Blimp in plus fours.

This was an image reinforced by TV when I was growing up. Many of the best *Two Ronnies* sketches were set in the nineteenth hole, drawing on the comic potential of a bunch of bank managers, regional sales directors, toothbrush moustaches and social ambition. Ronnie Corbett, Bruce Forsyth and Jimmy Tarbuck seemed to spend much of their downtime on the fairway at pro-am events. This mix of sport, comedy and Establishment gave golf an eccentric, exclusive aura.

Denis Thatcher was a perfect example of the amateur

golfer, a likeable old cove. Most of the preceding prime ministers' spouses had been content, or more likely obliged, to stay in the background – though Mary Wilson had turned her hand to poetry, which gave her a slightly higher profile than the rest. Denis was always going to be more media-worthy in any case, as the first man to play the supporting role at Number 10. Affably supportive, ever smiling, glasses twinkling and a G&T or three after a leisurely round at the golf club, he cleverly avoided impinging on his missus's political crusade. Even the spoof 'Dear Bill' letters, supposedly from Denis to Bill Deedes, which ran regularly in *Private Eye*, were sympathetic. If Maggie Thatcher was Mrs T, then Denis must have been the original Mr T, though the occasions when the A-Team could have usefully employed his anecdotes about bunker shots at Royal Lytham might have been few and far between.

I never thought I'd end up being a golfer. The local course in Stanmore was a very convenient adventure playground, a wonderful rolling landscape for amateur cross-country bike scrambles, war games or other nefarious activities. And the habit dies hard. At an end-of-filming wrap party, some of the cast and crew went on a bender of such majestic proportions that we were woken in the early morning, in various stages of hangover and undress, by angry posses of golfers disturbed to find alcohol-ridden corpses scattered across the second green.

But here I am, a card-carrying member of the Stage Golf Society, with a home in the genteel surroundings of Richmond Golf Club. It's the ideal sport for any actor –

when you're 'resting' you can stick the clubs in the back of the car and pop over for a round or two, and it's one of the few golf courses where you can overhear an interchange on the fairway along the lines of, 'Super shot, treasure' – 'Thank you, dear heart!' If the society ever needs a new motto, I might suggest this quote from Gary Player: 'If I had to choose between my wife and my putter . . . well, I'd miss her.'

Like tennis racquets, golf equipment has made vast leaps forward in terms of power and quality since the '70s. Cutting-edge clubs maximise their aerodynamic potential to hit balls that fly faster and further when you thwack them. One of the sweetest sights in amateur golf is the player who lovingly removes his Callaway Big Bertha from the bag, tenderly teases off its massive, cobra-like cover, caresses it for a while, addresses the ball (the latest one he saw in *Golf Monthly* that is guaranteed to increase his drive length by 10 per cent), takes a mighty swing, and promptly duckhooks it into the nearest coppice, never to be seen again.

Golf has always thrown up great and much-loved characters, perhaps because it's such an intense and personal sport. Although the greats are competing against the rest of the field, they are really playing against themselves and exposing their own flaws, their weaknesses and if possible their resolve in the face of everything nature and the course designer can throw at them, and with the close-up cameras of the world watching every drive, chip and putt. Even more so than snooker – every spring you would spend hours and days in intimate scrutiny of Hurricane

Higgins or Steve Davis – golf is the ultimate individual sport. So the legends of the '70s and '80s – the power of the 'Golden Bear' himself, Jack Nicklaus, the intensity of Arnold Palmer, the dark passion of Tony Jacklin and the wisecracking of Lee Trevino – were just as identifiable as Padraig Harrington, John Daly, Ian Poulter and Tiger Woods are today.

Tiger, at last and much overdue, began the process of breaching another of the sport's antiquated defences. As somebody once pointed out, fifty years ago a hundred white men chasing one black man across a field was called the Ku Klux Klan. And now? It's the US PGA tour.

Bovril crisps or pumpkin seeds

Snacks

30 June 1979 Trade publication *The Grocer* announces the launch by Smiths Crisps of pickled onion Monster Munch, the follow-up to the original roast beef flavour.

Crisps form one-third of the divine Holy Trinity of retro snacks, right up there with chocolate bars and fizzy drinks. Not as refreshing as a gulp of Cresta, certainly, not as comforting as a Cabana bar, perhaps, but for sheer hit-the-spot instant hunger relief they're hard to beat.

My generation was just the right age to appreciate the great 1970s crisp explosion. A major breakthrough in potato crisp technology – second only to inventing the things in the first place – was the arrival of the first flavoured varieties in 1962. This quantum leap in potatoid technology was courtesy of Golden Wonder and their cheese and onion crisps. Still a classic, of course, and what eating pleasure they must have brought to a generation whose crisp highlight had hitherto been unwrapping the twist of salt.

By the '70s, the next wave of flavours was ready to titillate the nation's taste buds – smoky bacon, prawn cocktail, salt and vinegar. More recently, there's been a lively debate, led most volubly by Harry Hill, about Walker's crisps and their colouring of packets. As Harry has pointed out, cheese and onion crisps should be in green packets, salt and vinegar in blue – not the other way round, as Walker's have it. (Only a cynic would suggest that they've done it deliberately so that crispophiles will get all hot, bothered and lightly salted about the whole question, and unwittingly give Walker's free plugs in best-selling books. Well, not in this one . . . oh, bollocks.)

Soon there was a new, even more glorious frontier of crisp tastes to be explored, and we were the willing guinea pigs busy consuming Bovril flavour, beef and onion, Worcester sauce, even the ultra-exotic paprika. Food technicians were working late into the night at Crisp HQ concocting combinations that would give Heston Blumenthal a gastronomic hard-on. They stopped short of creating the Quentin Crisp but that was about it. In those days the aim was to replicate good honest fare. Sausage and tomato sounds simple but it was an artistic masterpiece.

From then on, to be honest, it was a question of fine-tuning. Crisps can be made of beetroot, parsnips, whatever you like, but they're still crisps. You and I know that crumbly Red Windsor and shallot flavour is just a poncey packet of cheese and onion. Pumpkin or sunflower seeds? Not for me. Healthy as hell but, like tofu, no heft, no oomph. It reminds me of how kids were told that if you ate an orange pip it would take root in your stomach and a tree would grow out of your ears, nose and throat.

Jogging or spinning
Getting fit

15 September 1979 President Jimmy Carter, yellow headband and all, collapses during a light jog in Catoctin Mountain National Park. 'They had to drag me off,' he says. 'I didn't want to stop.'

Something I've recently remembered is the muscle man on *Opportunity Knocks*, who'd break out into a weird body-popping muscle display to the tune of 'Wagon Wheels', slathered in oil and looking like he'd stepped out of a very used deep-fat fryer. The other muscular role models of the day were the old-school wrestling superstars, before the grunt and groan of Geoff Capes in *The World's Strongest Man* and the pantomime antics of WWF: Jackie Pallo, Les Kellett and the camp one with gold trunks who used to hurl Giant Haystacks or Mick McManus – now Mick looked hard, but probably collected porcelain figurines in his spare time – on to the canvas and then flick his hair back.

Like stuntmen, fitness was for the professionals. Remember *Superstars*, when First Division footballers who were on twenty fags a day got run ragged by the really fit guys from judo or rowing? Terrific concept, and drama, like that moment when Kevin Keegan, one of the few footballers along with Malcolm MacDonald who did really well, crashed when racing a bike on a cinder track but staggered on. The music for *Superstars* was iconic. I tried to get it into *Ashes to Ashes* as well, for the scene when we were ploughing up the Thames in a motorboat armed to the gunwales, but we couldn't get that either.

There were always ads in the back of American magazines like *Mad!* for fun things like X-ray glasses or spy kits. And I'm thinking – but it can't be right, can it? – that they had bazookas too. Certainly there'd be an ad from Charles Atlas: 'You too can have a body like mine' . . . if you wanted to look like a complete tit with man breasts. And there were chest expanders, which allowed you to pose, look very silly and scream uncontrollably when they snapped back to catch your hair or, worse, your nipples in the springs.

When did fitness become all the rage? Maybe when jogging started in the '70s? Which in turn led to probably the most missed sporting activity – the mass streak. Streaking, what a great idea, taken to the peaks of perfection by Erica Roe at Twickenham.

Suddenly we were all getting fit. The '80s was the era of keep-fit videos – new technology then – with Jane Fonda in leotard and leggings, the Green Goddess and Mr Motivator on breakfast TV, and Princess Di nipping to the gym in her lunch break. Ever since, unused gym memberships have drained billions from the nation's bank accounts. Yoga, pilates, and best of all spinning classes – my God, those whirling dervishes must be fit.

The weird thing is that if you go into a gym now, the

men's locker room is like a male grooming salon. There are chaps in there who never make it into the actual gym area. They spend a couple of hours admiring themselves in the mirror, adjusting the towel for that supermodel look, exfoliating, scrubbing, buffing and preening, in a cloud of talc like the fallout from Krakatoa. By the time they've shaved their chest hair, gelled their head hair, and done Christ knows what with their scrotums, it's time for them to get dressed again. It's not right. Surely we need to bring back the heady aroma of liniment, athlete's foot powder and the sweaty jockstraps.

Mastermind or Sudoku

Brain fodder

15 December 1979 Trivial Pursuit is conceived by Canadian newspapermen Chris Haney and Scott Abbott, and the game is marketed two years later. In 1984 over twenty million sets would be sold.

The Mastermind I've got in mind is not the TV quiz show, the long-trouser version of *Top of the Form*, although Magnus Magnusson and his spotlit chair of interrogation were an unavoidable presence. No, this is the game that was always part of the Christmas holiday ritual, the one where you used tiny coloured pegs to create a code and your opponent had to crack it. Calling it Mastermind was a little ambitious. It was hardly Mensa territory – more of a cross between cribbage (something old people played), battleships and noughts and crosses, the perfect undemanding entertainment to while away a few hours between the Queen's Speech and *Morecambe and Wise*. The best part about the game was the box. There was a cover shot of a bearded guy in a wonderful suit and tie, an urbane John Virgo, deep in thought, with a willowy Chinese beauty standing behind him. He looked like one of James Bond's contacts from *You Only Live Twice*, but surely a crack intelligence agent was not wasting his time wondering which peg was the red one. He was probably far too busy choosing between chow mein or sweet and sour pork balls and egg fried rice.

When Trivial Pursuit came along in the early '80s, it tapped into the start of the pub quiz craze, guaranteed to clog up the last few memory cells still on active service with unusable factoids. Everyone always tried to avoid that green pie slice that forced you to answer the Science and Nature questions. There's a thin dividing line between general knowledge – the kind of stuff that might conceivably come in handy one day – and trivia. That's just factual binge-drinking, great wodges of data designed to block out the horror of daily life.

And now we've got Sudoku. I've never seen the appeal, although my old man is keen, so it's a skill that's obviously skipped a generation. A lot of actors love crosswords and Sudoku – Dean Andrews, a.k.a. DC Ray Carling, is a Sudoku whizz. Rather than exercising my brain muscles, I prefer to fill the downtime between takes by taking a nap. Wake me up before you go-go, Raymondo.

Shoot! or Nuts

Mags for boys

10 May 1980 This week's *Shoot!* contains posters of Frank Lampard (senior), Paul Mariner, Tommy Caton and Asa Hartford, and a piece on Martin Peters, the last 1966 World Cup winner still in First Division action at Norwich.

One of the highlights of the week for any sports-mad kid was the arrival of *Shoot!* magazine. Like most middle-aged gits, I first cut my magazine-reading teeth on comics, the *Beano* mainly, with Dennis the Menace, the Bash Street Kids and that well-known dealer to the animation world Billy Whizz – I knew he was fast, I just didn't realise he was sorted, guy. Occasionally you'd defect to *Whizzer and Chips*, or to one of those *Commando* books where our gallant lads took on Jerry in cartoon format – '*Donner und blitzen, Englander schweinehund!*'

I graduated from those to *Shoot!*, but only now do I realise how groundbreaking that magazine was: they'd run 'players at home' features with Martin Peters posing with his wife and kids in their new kitchen (actually paid for by themselves), or perching on a new Capri or Vauxhall Victor (also paid for by themselves). So *Shoot!* was the precursor, in its own way, of *Hello!* (even down to the exclamation mark) and *OK!*, whose pages are graced (if that's the right word) by the home lives and nuptials of our current crop of footie superstars. Now we know who to blame.

It wasn't just the glossy print quality and the photos that set *Shoot!* apart in its ongoing battle with *Match*. Footballers supplied regular columns and questionnaires, which their PR reps would never allow today. Joe Corrigan, the hefty Man City goalie, heartwarmingly chose 'toast' as his favourite food. Gerry Francis's favourite singer, intriguingly, was Captain Beefheart. And one of the most frequent answers to 'Most difficult opponent' was 'the ex-wife'.

The magazine was also a bit nerdy, with stats, a tactics section for trying out on chums' Subbuteo pitches and league ladders, which you could use to track the progress of all the teams using little card tabs. Most of us gave up by the end of September each season because it was too fiddly or the ladder disintegrated. Why would anyone bother nowadays, when massive tables of statistics, updated daily, are just a mouse click away?

Not surprisingly, *Shoot!* finally had to hang up its boots in June 2008, and is now running a pub in Hertfordshire. It was my first real boys' mag. I didn't have any sisters, so for those of you hoping for a dissection of the best of *Jackie* or *My Guy* – sorry, I can't help you. Ask the wife. The closest to a unisex magazine was *Look-In*, ITV's tie-in magazine, with features on the Osmonds, David Cassidy and the Bay City Rollers, and comic strips of shows from *Freewheelers*, *The Fonz* and *Catweazle* to *Charlie's Angels* and *The Bionic Woman*.

There were other magazines that punctuated growing up. *Smash Hits* was huge in the 1980s – the most famous member of the editorial team being Neil Tennant of the Pet Shop Boys – and there was also a raunchier German cousin, *Poptastik!* Then *Loaded* came along and later *Nuts* and *Zoo* – kind of *Viz* meets *Shoot!* but with revealing spreads of Page 3 babes instead of Kevin Keegan, his perm and his missus reclining in their new TV loungers.

The blokes' magazines sometimes ask me to appear in the odd macho article, usually talking cars. Generally I say no, because I'm not Gene Hunt. If I do pitch up for a car piece, some boy writer will invariably ask me what my first motor was. A Mini. 'Why?' says the petrolhead. 'Because it was all I could afford.' 'Oh, OK. So what did you move on to?' 'A Fiesta.' 'Ghia?' the writer enquires desperately, hoping I can help him out by boosting my blokish credentials. 'Yeah, definitely gears, five of them, reverse, top, the whole bloody lot.'

Juliet Bravo or Jane Tennison

TV policewomen

30 August 1980 The first episode of BBC's *Juliet Bravo*, written by Ian Kennedy Martin, the creator of *The Sweeney*, with Stephanie Turner in the title role as Inspector Jean Darblay.

The breakthrough policewoman series in the UK was *Juliet Bravo*, with Stephanie Turner as Inspector Jean Darblay. There had been policewomen on screen before but they were usually making the tea, treated as skivvies much like WPC Annie Cartwright, played by Liz White in *Life on Mars*. But in *Juliet Bravo* here was a female officer in charge of a testosterone-filled cop shop, taking control – and with a strangely convenient call sign, don't you think? I wonder what her male equivalent would have been. Maybe James Dreyfus as Constable Goody from *The Thin Blue Line* mincing into Hartley police station with his freshly assigned moniker: 'Hello, mam, I'm Romeo Foxtrot.'

The series was first shown in 1980, a period when equal opportunities were, if not exactly equal, then maybe slightly less unequal. When the chances of promotion were less dependent on a mirrored ceiling than breaking through the glass one. But it would be a long haul. The scene in *Ashes to Ashes* where Gene Hunt tells Alex Drake that she has to have her arse rubber-stamped seems far-fetched, but, believe me, I've been told by those in the know that this was just one of a whole raft of initiation ceremonies that took place in police forces across the country throughout the '70s and '80s.

Fan or stalker

You never can tell

8 December 1980 A few hours after signing a copy of his new album *Double Fantasy* for Mark Chapman, John Lennon is shot dead by Chapman in the entrance to the Dakota Building in New York.

When I was a kid, being a fan meant having a proper autograph book, a wodge of tightly bound pages, each in a different, though equally hideous, pastel shade. The whole point, believe it or not, was to collect the autographs of your idols and keep them, along with the memory of meeting whichever star it was, not to auction them off to the highest bidder before the ink had even dried. In fact, you'd keep the book so long that by the time you discovered it at the back of a drawer you had absolutely no idea who the scribbles were from – 'Who the fuck is that? Björn Borg?' (An exception to this rule is my wife, whose autograph book, featuring Morecambe and Wise alongside Judi Dench, is carefully notated on each page.)

My father was a TV director and as a birthday treat he might take me along to Television Centre in Wood Lane. The studios were turning out *Cilla, Are You Being Served?* and *Colditz*. We wandered through various tea bar-cum-green rooms, which back then offered stewed tea in polystyrene cups (now it's all Costa Coffee and Starbucks franchises). The old man pointed out Robert Wagner, David McCallum, and Major Pat Reid, the genuine escapee who was advising on the show. Finally we came across Anthony Valentine, who played the Nazi officer Major Horst Mohn of the SS – you remember, the one with the bayonet scar down the side of his face, think Action Man (or Herr Aktion?) – relaxing with a cuppa and a Dunhill. 'Hello, Johnny, how the devil are you?' he said. Another autograph in the bag.

My nerve failed me, though, when my father took me and Paterson down the corridors to knock on Spike Milligan's door. Paul and I proffered our autograph books with a 'Sorry to bother you, Spike' but it was not one of Spike's better days. 'Not the way to do this, mutter, mutter' – so sadly I have no brilliant Milligan epigrams to regale you with. I have to confess I bottled out at that point, but Paterson hung in there in the face of Spike's curmudgeonly wrath and got his autograph – shove it on eBay, kid!

These days, the mobile phone allows fans to operate from a distance. During the first day's filming for the second series of *Life on Mars*, John Simm and I were outside the very '60s/'70s Stockport Town Hall. When we'd done the same on the first series, of course nobody had really taken much notice (probably because we weren't in *Corrie*), but this time round, after John and I finished the opening scene, we looked up and there was somebody at every window and all down the long stairwells, pointing their camera phone at us.

Fan or stalker

I've now worked out a foolproof system for spotting the 'ardent fans' who are hoping to turn a quick buck. They send in letters along the lines of 'Dear Mr Glenister/Mr Craig/Mr McGregor [please delete as appropriate], I have been a fan of yours since your first appearance as a nuclear blast victim in *Casualty*/lowly PC on *The Bill*/chirpy stall-holder on *EastEnders* [please delete as appropriate], and have watched the entire DVD collection of . . .' You get the idea.

When I do take a sneaky peek at eBay, the autographs purporting to be mine are so ridiculously different from my own, it's unbelievable. They don't even make an attempt at forgery. I guess that since Colditz and the other Stalags closed down, the artisans who rendered passports and transit papers with just half a potato and a blunt needle have gone the way of cordwainers, fletchers and scriveners.

Kentucky Fried Chicken or KFC

Rebranding

16 December 1980 Harland Sanders, the self-styled Colonel, dies. Allegedly, all the flags on Kentucky state buildings fly at half mast for four days.

There was a time when Kentucky Fried Chicken was completely upfront about being fried. When the goateed Colonel would pop up in TV ads and proudly slurp a glob of good ol' secret-recipe grease off every digit. They even told you in the strapline that it was 'finger-lickin' good'.

We all knew what the deal was. This was chicken and it was fried, and the recipe for the coating came from Kentucky. No problem. A party bucket was basically a gallon of lovely, greasy, fried chicken. That's precisely why we bought it. We're fried, say it with pride.

Then what happens? Come the early 1990s and Kentucky Fried Chicken go all coy. They turn into KFC. Like some highfalutin accountants. Maybe they wanted to align themselves with Kilmarnock Football Club. Or perhaps we were meant to imagine there was now a more sophisticated cooking technique and that F now stood for fricasséed or flambéed. It made not one iota of difference as to whether we walked on past their restaurants or bagged yet another bucket. Apparently KFC have now got the message, because they are rumoured to be thinking about reverting to Kentucky Fried Chicken.

But they had already unleashed a huge trend for rebranding. Everybody was at it, especially now we were part of a massive global market. Marathon became Snickers, Opal Fruits turned into Starburst. (Remember the Opal Fruits ad? 'Fresh with the tang of citrus. Four refreshing fruit flavours – Orange! Lemon! Strawberry! Lime!') Labour? We'll call it New Labour. Even trade unions got in on the act, redubbing themselves Unison or Connect – and the Wheeltappers and Shunters' Union would from now on like to be known as Touchy-Feely.

A short note to my rebranding consultants: re your suggestion that I should henceforth and in perpetuity change my name from Philip Haywood Glenister to PHG – please F. O.

Bell bottoms or sarong

Fashion victims

24 January 1981 Adam Ant sports Vivienne Westwood's piratical New Romantic look as the Ants' album, *Kings of the Wild Frontier*, including the singles 'Antmusic', 'Dog Eat Dog' and the title track, reaches UK Number One.

Fashion choices are intensely personal and, unlike woodchip wallpaper, each successive trend vanishes almost before it's started. I once spent so long looking in army surplus stores for exactly the right battered leather flying jacket that by the time I found one they were well out of fashion.

There was what we used to call the Budgie jacket, as worn by Adam Faith in the TV series, the two-tone, zip-up bomber jacket with the big round collar and lapels. That outfit links with the Danny Wilde look in *The Persuaders* of belted jacket, scarf and open-backed tan leather driving gloves: note my little homage to Tony with Gene Hunt's gloves.

At school, just as kids do now, we spent an immense amount of time messing around with our ties, trying to create the biggest knot.

As far as fashion for girls was concerned, I was an interested (and sometimes bemused) observer. (I loved the

Afghan coat and hot pants ensemble.) In the '80s various trends swept across our vision: the Princess Di frills and flounces, that Joan Collins power-dressing look, the Madonna puffball skirt, multi-zipped flying suits, and a brief phase (for which I will always hold Sheena Easton personally responsible) when I only ever seemed to meet girls in waistcoats. It was like going out with Hurricane Higgins.

Cliff or Scooch

Nul points

4 April 1981 The United Kingdom win Eurovision, held in Dublin that year, with Bucks Fizz and 'Making Your Mind Up', courtesy of a (deliberate) wardrobe malfunction.

I almost forgot to include Eurovision, but how could I possibly leave out such a nostalgia touchstone? Problem is, these days it's impossible for the UK to win against the Brit-hating massed ranks of Eastern Europe and the old USSR. It's all very different from the days when Lulu or Sandie or Cliff or Olivia travelled to foreign parts to defend our honour in song. (By the way, what was Olivia doing representing us? She's a bloody Australian. But Australia's part of the Commonwealth, so sod it – she's in.)

Things have come to a pretty pass when the best Scooch could do was celebrate getting more than *nul points*. There was once a decent prospect of the UK coming away with the top prize. Sandie Shaw had proved it could be done even if she forgot to pack her shoes with 'Puppet on a String' in 1967, and Lulu had shared the honours two years later in a four-way tie, giving her 'Boom Bang-a-Bang'.

But try as he might, the future Sir Cliff couldn't match

the girls. 'Congratulations' was pipped to the post in 1968 by Spain's 'La La La'. Cliff took a second stab in 1973 in Luxembourg, looking like a cross between a page boy and Jeff Beck, and doing the most ridiculously camp moves imaginable to 'Power to All Our Friends'. He only made third. The winner that year? The host country's Anne-Marie David with 'Tu Te Reconnaîtras'. No, I can't remember it either. Thank Christ ABBA blasted in with 'Waterloo' in 1974 – by some distance the best song to emerge from the whole extravaganza.

Now, thanks to a Spanish documentary team, we learn that apparently Cliff woz robbed. A fiendish Francoist plot engineered victory for 'La La La' at the expense of 'Congratulations'. And just after that story broke, Spain swept to the Euro 2008 trophy and Rafa Nadal finally beat Federer at Wimbledon. Coincidence? I wonder how many people promptly nipped out to the bookies and put a wodge on Sergio Garcia finally to win a major. 'Ding Ding-a-Dong'.

'You cannot be serious' or Hawkeye

New balls, please

4 July 1981 On Independence Day, Super Brat John McEnroe beats Björn Borg to win the Wimbledon men's title, 4–6, 7–6, 7–6, 6–4.

Borg. McEnroe. Connors. When men were men (including several of the women), racquets were wooden, serve and volley was the order of the day, and disputed line calls could not be settled by computer simulation. If Hawkeye had been around in 1981, we would have been denied the joy of watching McEnroe deliver his perfectly petulant one-liners, and that would have been a great tragedy.

Unlike McEnroe and co., things were always far too quiet on the British tennis front, which was, inevitably, bumping along in its own furrow of mediocrity. We were already looking back to Roger Taylor, the beetle-browed left-hander who had made the semi-finals of Wimbledon a few times in the late '60s and early '70s. And even then Fred Perry's trio of titles in the mid-1930s seemed part of ancient history, from a lost, sepia-toned pre-war era. A youthful Sue Barker had picked up the French Open in 1976, and a pink-cardiganed Virginia Wade had grabbed the Wimbledon title in the centenary year of 1977, thrilling that half of the nation who were celebrating the Queen's Silver Jubilee rather than listening to the Pistols.

After that, though, success was rare. Annabel Croft couldn't hack it on the pro tour. Various nearly men and women came and went: remember Jo Durie? Then Tiger Tim did his best to get us overexcited. And now Andy Murray – you really need a nickname, my son – has been doing the same. But a quiet word, Andy, don't flex your biceps on Centre Court again. Rafa Nadal can do it because he's got a Balearically bronzed superbody. Just go out and win the bastard thing first before the media bring you down, as they most surely will. Ditto Laura Robson – don't let them big you up too soon, Laura.

Is it any wonder the press get hyped up every time there's a whiff of tennis success? It's because there hasn't been a British singles champion since speech was invented. It's all part of that depressing trend where us Brits have invented the great world sports – footie, cricket, rubgy – just to watch everyone else do them ten times better. As the Australians pointed out during the Olympics – we only seem to excel at sports these days if we're sitting down – rowing, sailing, cycling . . . Someone pass Murray the umpire's chair!

Bubble car or Smart car

Odd little motors

8 September 1981 The first showing of John Sullivan's *Only Fools and Horses*, starring Del Boy's 1972 Robin Reliant Regal Superior van, the flagship of Trotters Independent Trading Co.

If you ever need to give a French acquaintance conclusive proof that les Rosbifs are completely bonkers – they will already suspect this, based on our penchant for Marmite and driving on the left – then take them to see a Morris Minor Traveller. The sight of a half-timbered thatched cottage on wheels will clinch it, and send them into a paroxysm of shrugs, '*incroyables*' and pitying glances.

The tarmac of yesteryear was pounded by a fleet of odd little cars. The Traveller was definitely a one-off, so left-field that if it had been designed now, you'd think it was a wacky promotional idea for creosote or double-glazing.

The Robin Reliant three-wheeler not only looked as if it was about to topple over at the slightest bend but was legendarily slow. Jasper Carrott had a sketch where he played a traffic copper taking the details of a Robin as it inched past. 'Did you get the registration number?' 'Yeah,' said Jasper, '*and* the chassis number.' There were also three-wheelers for the disabled which looked like a cross between a Robin and a Dalek, which you could see parked at one end of Stamford Bridge on match days.

Some small cars were funky, though. The Fiat Cinquecento was tiny but had enough residue of *la dolce vita* about it to be considered a style icon in the same way a Citroën 2CV had Gallic flair. And the Mini came complete with the smart cultural heritage of the Monte Carlo Rally (Scalextric even had a special Mini Rally set), *The Italian Job* and leggy birds from the King's Road.

I've saved the best of these motors till last. The bubble car. Haven't seen one on the road for many a year. Perhaps they're no longer street legal. Many of them were built by Heinkel and Messerschmitt, which explained why the bubble looked like the cockpit of a bomber popped on to a few bits of left-over undercarriage. Didn't even have a steering wheel – just a joystick.

As car design has become more homogeneous, it's good to see there's still room for quirky small vehicles – the various Smart cars, and the G-Wiz, which you hook up to the mains overnight (golf carts for city folk). Though, as the joke goes, you'd need a bloody long extension lead to get you round the M25.

David Vine or Hazel Irvine

Sports commentators

9 September 1981 Commentator Bjørge Lillelien celebrates Norway's 2–1 defeat of England in a World Cup qualifier in Oslo: 'Can you hear me, Maggie Thatcher? Your boys took one hell of a beating!'

Great sports commentators only have to say a couple of words for maximum impact. David Coleman was the master of minimalism. 'Hughes . . . Keegan . . . Toshack. One–nil.' Dan Maskell could sum up an entire rally with 'That's a dream of a volley . . .'

On hazy summer evenings, the gentle deliveries of Richie Benaud, Johnners and John Arlott could ease the pain of England being lashed by the West Indies. On muddy Sunday afternoons in winter, Brian Moore or one of the regional *Big Match* commentators, maybe Gerald Sinstadt covering the Bolton–Blackburn derby, were as succinct as Coleman. And each sport had commentators who combined real knowledge with great personality: Murray Walker during the F1 season; Peter Alliss and Henry Longhurst on golf; Eddie Waring for rugby league; Cliff Morgan and Bill McLaren during the Five Nations ('They'll be dancing in the streets of Galashiels'); Harry Carpenter at ringside. Each year Raymond Brooks-Ward encouraged the riders in the Horse of the Year Show ('Come on, Harvey') as they attempted the puissance, the kamikaze version of showjumping when the wall would get higher and higher until the more sensible horses said, 'Bollocks to this!', threw their riders, and buggered off for a fresh bale of hay. And during the World Snooker Championship Ted Lowe's tone was forever hushed, like he was auditioning for *EastEnders*.

Almost every sport now has a specialist commentator and a summariser who's performed at international level, but back then David Vine, Ron Pickering or Barry Davies used to head off to cover the more obscure sports after a quick flick through the *Observer Book of Curling* or *I-Spy Ski-Jumping*, in the sure knowledge that most viewers knew even less than they did. Most of the legends have now departed. Stuart Hall's mellifluous whimsy still occasionally enlivens Radio Five Live (surely a candidate for national treasure, if only for his uncontrollable laughter during *It's a Knockout*), but even Motty is finally hanging up his microphone. In his heyday, female commentators were virtually unknown – maybe Virginia Wade might have been invited to say a few words during the Ladies' Final at Wimbledon. But thankfully there are many more of them now, freshening up a genre that was in danger of being swamped by hordes of anonymous, sound-alike male commentators – although Alan Green, Martin Tyler and Andy Gray are honourable exceptions.

Sid Waddell is still producing some wonderful turns of phrase for the darts, wringing remarkable metaphors out of a game that follows a predictable treble 20, treble 20,

double top pattern in almost every leg. Sid must have contributed greatly to darts' huge popularity, which peaked
around the time of *Bullseye*. Peter Kay has a good routine
about this: he reckons the producers must have had a
brother-in-law with a boatyard, so often did a speedboat
emerge from behind the curtains as the star prize. It was
just a shame that the winners came from Tamworth, two
hundred miles from the nearest sea.

A–Z or sat nav

Lost and found

12 January 1982 News breaks that Mark Thatcher, son of Maggie, has got lost while taking part in the Paris–Dakar Rally. He will never live it down.

Somewhere along the way we've lost the ability to read a map. What's so difficult about it? This is not the 'Men are from Mars, women couldn't read a map if their life depended on it' debate. I don't want to take a wrong turn down that particular cul-de-sac, thank you very much. No, this is about the simple art of looking at an A–Z and know-ing exactly where you are. Or scanning a new road atlas – in that nanosecond before the numbers change and you're obliged to buy the next edition – and realising that taking the second left that goes directly to the hotel is preferable to turning right and ending up in a canal. Those basic ori-enteering skills.

You could spend hours as a kid poring over Ordnance Survey maps. Oh yes, my friend, you won't catch me mis-taking a church with a square tower for one with a spire in a hurry, no way. What I always wondered was why the maps marked post offices. Did the cartographers imagine we'd all be shooting along the A12 and suddenly think, 'Shit, I forgot to apply for a new passport. Can you track down a post office pronto, love?' It made about as much sense as those odd couples who would drive for two hours to the seaside, park up on the prom and sit in the car in their Pac-a-Macs with a thermos and some Spam sandwiches, never once getting out for a lungful of ozone, before heading all the way back home again, sucking on a Callard & Bowser.

In the '70s Clark's came out with a shoe called Commandos. They had a compass hidden inside the shoe, just underneath the heel. Great equipment for a crack sabotage platoon. 'OK, Sergeant, we're going to give Jerry hell tonight. What's our location?' 'Oooh, sorry, sir, I can't get my laces undone. What was it again? Was it the bunny ears first?' I can't remember if it was those shoes which also had embossed animal hoof- and paw-prints on the sole, one footprint for a deer, a badger and a few other woodland creatures, just in case you ever needed to track a one-legged stoat.

In the absence of a pair of Commandos, I can't see what's so difficult about sticking with maps. The sat nav in my last car was so sophisticated that it got cocky. Coming back from Beaconsfield one day, it steered me off the carriageway and up a police sliproad, the bitch. I leave the sat nav turned off now. What gets to me most is not the misdirection but the unctuous tones of the speaking voice. It's totally unrealistic because it lacks all the naked aggression of the usual husband-and-wife map-reading interface.

Someone should come up with a sat nav containing a reality voice over. 'Make a U-turn . . . you twat.' That's it. Twat nav. This could be a winner. See you on *Dragon's Den*.

Players No. 6 or Niquitin

Smoking

9 July 1982 Michael Fagan manages to get inside Buckingham Palace and reaches the Queen's private apartments. He is only caught when he asks HM for a cigarette, allowing her to phone for help. He was asking the wrong sister, of course. Mags would have 'borrowed' him one, for sure.

One of the most visible differences between twenty or thirty years ago and today is the change in attitudes to smoking, especially since the ban kicked in at the end of June 2007. I come from a family of smokers, as did most people in the '70s.

Everybody in the house smoked: mum, dad, grand-parents. During the Christmas Day meal, the grown-ups would light up between courses. As soon as the turkey was cleared away, out would come the fags. The big old lighter on its onyx base was brought in, and a smog would settle over the table until it was time for the pud to be served.

The anti-smoking message didn't get much of an airing on TV, even kids' TV: remember Lady Penelope taking an elegant drag through her ciggie holder on *Thunderbirds*? Try that in 2008 and Gerry Anderson would be banged up like Parker in his prison fatigues. And what about sweet cigarettes for a bit of subliminal brainwashing: one brand even had Superman on the packet, even though he was simultaneously fighting the dastardly Nick-O-Teen elsewhere!

I can't remember my first cigarette, it's lost in the haze. But I reckon it must have been a Guards, because that was what one of my friends' dads smoked, and he had a flip-top silver cigarette box recessed into one of the tables in the living room, yet another glamorous addition to the paraphernalia of smoking.

Each brand of cigarette had an image to go with it. Along with Guards, there was Senior Service, the kind of fags Second (and First) World War veterans could be proud of. Players No. 6 was the bog-standard choice. For a bit of Formula One glamour the sleek, black John Player Special sent out a message of pseudo-sophistication that was different from the smoky snooker halls that Embassy suggested. Park Drive or Fribourg & Treyer offered a touch of class. After a trip to Calais, we sported Gitanes, Gauloises or Camels, if your throat and lungs could take it. And TV played its part: Kojak fans preferred Mores to copy his brand of slender brown cigarettes, and maybe moved on to lollipops too.

There is no hierarchy now: just smoker or non-smoker. If you want a fag you have to stand shivering on a street corner like an old tart. Let's face it – smokers these days are about as welcome as George W. Bush on a state visit to . . . well, anywhere.

8-track or MP3

Music formats

1 October 1982 In one of the critical turning points of audio technology, Sony launch the CD on the Japanese market.

The 33 r.p.m. vinyl LP had many upsides. The covers were thin enough to allow you to squeeze hundreds of them on to a shelf, but wide enough to read the name of the album, which meant that you could gauge the taste of any new mate or potential girlfriend in a matter of seconds by scanning the spines. The sleeve, especially the double gatefold, was a perfect canvas for graphic designers and had enough space to print the whole album's lyrics plus some random liner notes, just enough to read on the bus journey home from the record store as you waited and waited to drop the needle on to the vinyl.

The downsides involved those needles scratching straight across the album that had been so carefully brought back, ruining it for ever, and the twenty-minutes-per-side format, which had you hopping up to turn to Side B just when you were in the middle of some intricate fore-play.

The LP was champion for a long time, happily co-existing with the 45 single and later the 12-inch single (i.e. a great hit track on one side, flip it over and you can listen to twelve non-stop hours of the backing track). Challenges from other formats came and went. There was a brief period in the mid-'70s when quadraphonic sound was being touted as the way forward, but it soon became clear that the dramatic difference between mono and stereo was only slightly enhanced by having two more speakers. The chunky 8-track car stereo – although now a collector's item – was just *too* chunky. So it was left to the audio cassette to find a niche as the most portable format, the one you could use in a car, and, since you could record on to a blank cassette, the format to blame for a thousand party compilations. The first Sony Walkmans, the size of a brick, started trickling into the UK in 1980, and suddenly the biggest problem with vinyl was highlighted – to play an album, you needed half a ton of equipment.

The CD revolution that had taken place by the end of the '80s allowed record companies to make pots of money by reissuing everything in their vaults, and the poor sods whose shelves were groaning with vinyl had to decide whether it was worth spending vast fortunes to recreate their collections in this new digital format. We'd just about made all those decisions, replenished the shelves, in fact gone out and bought brand-new, customised storage towers from IKEA, when the MP3 and iPod *coup d'état* made the CD look very old hat.

Now you can locate and download music in seconds, there's no need for bus journeys to record shops and lengthy discussions with surly assistants because you can't remember the exact title of the album you want. These days twelve-year-olds have bigger music libraries than the most avid collector possessed in the 1970s. But how much music can any one person listen to in a lifetime? The reality is that getting older is not about losing your bloody memory. It's just that there are so many bloody things to remember.

Mullet or slaphead

Haircuts (100)

20 October 1982 'Wishing (If I Had a Photograph of You)' hits the record stores. It becomes a Top Ten hit for A Flock of Seagulls, whose Mike Score, a former hairdresser, sports one of the weirdest hairstyles of the '80s.

There was a wonderful track on *Derek and Clive (Live)*, the album capturing the surreal stream of consciousness interplay between Peter Cook and Dudley Moore that came out in 1976. It was called 'The Worst Job I Ever Had' and essentially had Clive (Peter) declaring that his worst career was 'retrieving lobsters from Jayne Mansfield's bum' and Derek (Dudley) countering that his was 'collecting Winston Churchill's bogies'.

I should call this section 'The Worst Haircut I Ever Had'. It was in the early 1980s. This was a phase when every other pupil leaving school became a trainee hairdresser. I had a friend who became one, and for some reason this also meant he had to wear leather trousers. He practised on his friends, and the haircut he devised for me was somewhere between a Mohican, a mullet and the worst of the New Romantics. I looked like a new species of tree.

My haircuts had previously been courtesy of the

Spiders Web salon. The name alone should have been a clue. They could not have been proper hairdressers, since there was no obvious pun involved. Everyone knows all pukka hair salons should be called Curl Up and Dye, Shear Ecstasy or Beyond the Fringe.

The second thing about the Spiders Web was that the guys who ran it were their own worst advert. One looked like a reject from the Quo, complete with denim jacket and cheesecloth shirt – in fact, he was the spit of Justin Lee Collins – while his partner in crimp bore a remarkable resemblance to Bill Werbeniuk, the Canadian snooker player who legendarily downed eight pints of lager to prepare for every match and then one more for each frame. On the basis that you should take a good look at your stylists' hairstyle before deciding whether you want to let them loose on your own barnet (or even your own wealdstone), it was not one of my best decisions.

At least I managed to avoid the the worst excesses of the much-maligned Michael Bolton mullet – watch a rerun of the Band Aid recording session and you can see a glorious selection of mullets on display, from Bono to Paul Young – the reverse mullet (the 'tellum') and the Cure-style New Wave backcomb, what *Smash Hits* might have called a 'fright wig'.

Incidentally, there's a hairdresser in Seven Sisters with the most reassuring name ever. It's called It *Will* Grow Back.

Chopper or Segway

Getting around

9 December 1982 E.T.: The Extra-Terrestrial is released in the UK, with its memorable image of Elliott and E.T. on Elliott's Kuwahara BMX bike flying across the face of the moon.

The bicycle was something of a status symbol in the '70s. The choice of bike, and your ability to persuade your parents to shell out on the one you really wanted, was a yardstick of standing among your chums.

One major decision was between the Raleigh Chopper and a racing bike. I chose a racer – or it chose me – seduced by that sleek beast look, and the old man found a top-notch second-hand beauty. And boy, I looked after it so carefully. I knew how to get the chain back on, and all the tricks for finding and fixing punctures – if there wasn't a bowl of water handy, I could track down the split by spitting gob on the tyre and squeezing it until I found the tear. Not exactly classy. But practical. If a plastic football landed on a rose bush, you could simply heat a spoon on an electric hob and press it over the hole to melt the plastic back together, getting a few third-degree burns along the way. Those knacks, along with inserting flicker cards in the bike spokes, have gone the way of darning socks: try and mend a puncture now? Forget it. Where's the nearest bike shop?

So why didn't I go for the Chopper? It was cool in a lo-tech *Easy Rider* kind of way, with those high handlebars and the padded, lean-back seat. Great colours: fiery reds, oranges and yellows, metallic blue. There was even one with exhaust flames spurting down the back fork, perfect for attempting Evel Knievel stunts in the back garden, but, and it's a big but, that stubby gear lever in the middle of the crossbar was naff. You knew it made no difference at all, only there for show.

Bikes were only one of our transportation options. Back then, we would spend hours, days, constructing go-carts from the bits and bobs we scrounged off parents and neighbours or nicked from building sites: old pram wheels, discarded planks, bits of string for rudimentary steering. We were the original Scrapheap Challengers, constructing fantastic vehicles out of nothing, recycling like crazy, and then careering down the steepest hill you could find, totally reckless. And when the snows came, as they seemed to every December and January back in the '70s – aye, we had proper winters back in them thare days, my lad – the wooden toboggan would be disinterred from the back of the garage. Of course, it had never been looked after all year, so the runners were rusty, and would leave great rust-red tyre marks in its wake.

There was an endless choice of self-propelled vehicles, from roller-skates and scooters to the Spacehopper – a triumph – and the pogo-stick. And stilts! Kids used to totter around on wooden stilts like escapees from Billy Smart's Circus. This was a childhood spent outdoors, from eight in the morning to eight at night during the summer holidays, with no PS3 to play, and not much more than one hour of kids' TV. You weren't a true kid of the '70s until your knees were properly bruised and scabbed up. Think Chopper Harris.

After the BMX revolution, the next two-wheel development, apart from those terrifying bicycles you have to ride while lying flat on your back, and the mini metal scooters for grown-up kids, was the Segway – that futuristic electric two-wheeler you stand on, like riding along the back axle of a car with handlebars.

Not sure about the Segway. Although it has more urban cachet than the Sinclair C5 ever could, you'd still look like a little kid who's got lost buzzing up the A1 on one. I see a lot of them because film crews started using them as an alternative to tracking shots. Instead of rigging up a Clapham Junction's-worth of track on set, the cameraman can hitch himself to a Steadycam and roll alongside on his Segway, although how the hell they can see where they're going and look through the eyepiece at the same time I have no idea. On *Life on Mars* there was one scene where the crew planned to use a Segway, but it was on a cobbled street. Doesn't work, lads, impossible, think about it . . . So they had to build a track specially for the Segway, which pretty much defeated the whole object of using it in the first place.

Tufty Club or speed cameras

Road safety

31 January 1983 Compulsory wearing of seat belts for drivers and front-seat passengers comes into force in the UK.

Safety on foot and on bikes was drilled into my generation by a succession of school visits from local coppers, road-safety officers, Green Cross Code men and lollipop ladies, full of good advice on how to cross a road.

There's been a change of emphasis from the simple delights of the Tufty Club (Tufty was like a distant cousin of Tingha and Tucker). Look at road safety ads now. They're all aimed at the drivers, with slow-mo shots of kids bouncing off car bonnets and enough post-trauma fakery to keep the *Casualty* and *Holby City* make-up teams in work for years. What the road safety bods must have realised is that you can spend as much time as you like telling kids to look left, right and left again, and installing flashing green men across the country, but all this won't make a blind bit of frigging difference if the nob-end at the wheel of his 4x4 is texting his bit of fluff as he completely ignores another pedestrian crossing.

You didn't have to wear a seat belt at all until 1983, and it was still legal for kids to be unbelted in the back until 1989. 'Clunk click every trip' was only a suggestion, not compulsory for a long time. Dangerous, of course, but it did mean you could lie flat out on the back seat all the way back from Devon, snoozing gently next to a pile of *I-Spy* books while smartly dressed AA and RAC officers saluted the passing car.

Drivers were pretty unrestricted – no sleeping policemen, speed bumps or cameras – and at night they were doubtless three powerful Irish coffees to the wind at a time when drinking and driving was almost acceptable. And the cars themselves were much less safe too, with no SIPS or air bags. When they crashed the results were usually gruesome. I recently watched a bunch of post-war public information films on road safety released around the time that the M1 was opened. 'Oh, Brian, we seem to be going the wrong way.' 'No, we're not darling.' 'Yes, we appear to be heading on to the motorway against the flow of the traffic.' 'Now, don't worry, Marjorie, I know perfectly well what I'm doing.' Cue screeching tyres followed by mass explosion.

Jason King or soul beard

Facial fungus

23 March 1983 The album *Eliminator* – including 'Gimme All Your Lovin" and 'Legs' – is released by ZZ Top, whose drummer Frank Beard is famously the only band member without a gigantic beard.

Jason King, the dapper, champagne-loving international sleuth, spy and seducer played by Peter Wyngarde, and the inspiration for Mike Myers' Austin Powers, was a fashion explosion. Bespoke velvet suits with waistcoat and fob chain, lurid silk shirt with matching tie, massive collar and cuffs which he turned up outside his suit, and hair and sideburns coiffed into a rigid helmet. He even wore a kaftan at one point! But the final touch – the last detail that turned him from what Bill Bryson once called 'a ridiculous rake whom women unaccountably appeared to find alluring' into a 1970s icon – was the moustache.

This was a classic of the times. A cross between a handlebar, a Frank Zappa and a Zapata, a bristling declaration of such hetero pulling power that when Wyngarde was busted for cottaging in the mid-'70s, it was a scandal of George Michael proportions. Alongside the Freddie Mercury/Village People 'tache, the ZZ Top beards and the old-school stylings of Terry-Thomas, Jimmy Edwards and

Bruce Forsyth, I have to mention the Liverpool FC moustache. It was a constant feature of all the great Anfield sides of the era – Rush, Souness, Grobbelaar, even Lawro all sporting them like Samson (if not Kenny Sansom), as a badge of pride and a source of strength.

The gallery of facial hairstyles on offer to the pubescent child of the '70s and '80s – strange word, 'pubescent': if you look at it long enough it turns into 'pube scent'! – included the 'entrepreneur' look of Richard Branson, a neat and tidy beard that found its expression on prime-time TV in the form of Noel Edmonds and Jeremy Beadle. I could include the Bee Gees' beards in that category too. Noel, of course, has had the same style since time immemorial. It's almost impossible to imagine him without it – in fact, it would be bloody horrendous. As horrendous as when Branson dressed as a bride. The stuff of nightmares.

Moon Unit or Dwayne

Names for children

31 March 1983 Bob Geldof, at this point still an ex-Boomtown Rat rather than a living saint, and Paula Yates, presenter on *The Tube*, celebrate the birth of their first daughter, Fifi Trixibelle.

The underlying trends for naming children continue to evolve through the decades, as tracked by *The Times* each year – although the paper's sampling used to be slightly skewed since it was based on the Births announcements in its own pages, hardly a sociologically valid reflection of Britain. Nevertheless, the names often reflected a celebrated public figure's appearance in the public consciousness. That's why the '50s and '60s saw a clutch of Philips – in the wake of the arrival of Phil the Greek who captured a young princess's heart.

But, dear God, even the highly trained reserve of HM must have been under extreme pressure when she heard that Peter Phillips was bringing a radiant bride called Autumn into the family, knowing as she did that there was already a Chelsy waiting in the wings for young Harry. When placed alongside the *Hello!*-funded wedding cele-brations – although the astute old bird might well have grudgingly approved of such pragmatism – it seemed that the royal family was moving into *Footballers' Wives* territory. Less House of Windsor, more World of Leather. Deep in the back of the regal mind, did she feel a shudder of apprehension as she looked forward to a line of succession full of tiny Princess Chardonnays and Prince Romeos waving to the crowds from the balcony at HQ?

Offbeat names have always been around. The early '70s saw some corking coinages spun by the hippy generation. A tab of acid on the way to the register office had some surprising results. From that era, high-profile names included Zowie Bowie and the Frank Zappa kids, Moon Unit, Dweezil and Diva Thin Muffin Pigeon. A decade later came Bob Geldof and Paula Yates, whose Fifi Trixibelle comfortably romped home to win the most ridiculous name of the '80s. The torch was then handed on to the Beckhams for their midfield trio of Brooklyn, Romeo and Cruz. Posh and Becks announced at the time of Brooklyn's birth that they'd chosen the name because he'd been conceived there. Just as well they didn't get a bit frisky walking down Peckham High Street.

Clap or chlamydia
STDs

5 April 1983 Thrush is finally defeated, but only as the power-crazed organisation T.H.R.U.S.H in *The Return of the Man from U.N.C.L.E.*, a one-off reunion of Robert Vaughn and David McCallum.

At the end of the all-too-brief window in the '70s and '80s, virtually every girl was on the pill, and sexual diseases seemed a distant threat. They all had short, brutish names, and were grouped together under the distinctly unpleasant-sounding VD – the clap, crabs and scabies, which still sounded positively Victorian, even though the Damned's drummer used it for half of his stage name (but then I guess Christopher Miller didn't have quite the same ring as Rat Scabies). We reckoned these diseases were only likely to be picked up by the Merchant Navy.

By the mid-'80s, the window was crashing shut, with the first alarm bells ringing about AIDS, and the subsequent awareness of a whole new and disturbing set of STDs. Chlamydia? It sounds like a plant for the garden, just next to your laburnum. No, ta. No wonder Boy George suggested a nice cup of tea instead.

Trimphone or Crazy Frog

Hanging on the telephone

13 June 1983 The first mobile phone to hit the market is released in the US: the Motorola DynaTAC 8000X. Known as 'the brick', it retailed for $3,995.

In those dim, distant years before I 'crept the boards in my youth' (as Uncle Monty from *Withnail & I* put it), I worked for a while as a film publicist (and not a very good one, I hasten to add). One of the movies I worked on was *The Fourth Protocol* in 1987, and Freddie Forsyth, who'd written the novel, was in London to help with promotion. We'd organised a press screening at the Odeon Leicester Square, and at one point I looked across the foyer to see Freddie striding about and talking into a huge phone, with wires disappearing into a petrol tank that he was lugging around. He was barking into the thing in a Freddie Forsyth kind of way. By the time he rang off and put this bloody great case down, he looked like he'd dislocated his shoulder. With hindsight, this telecommunications beast was laughably gigantic, but at the time it was dead impressive.

The telecommunications revolution was nigh. And that meant the beginning of the end for the public phone box. No more could you spend hours collecting 2ps and 10ps to weigh down the pockets of your finest flares, before standing politely outside the nearest red phone box, waiting for the guy inside to finish an interminable conversation with his girlfriend, and then snapping once your patience wore out, banging on the door to tell him to get a move on, for Chrissakes. How many crucial, emotionally charged conversations were cut off in mid-angst as the pips went and there were no 2ps left?

You could always try asking the operator to reverse the charges, though the inherent risk was hearing your loved one telling the operator, 'No way', because she never wanted to speak to you again. Public humiliation and heartbreak, accompanied by the next bloke in the queue banging on the door and telling *you* to get a friggin' move on.

At home, the heavy-duty round-dial phone was the standard issue one doled out to homes along with cheap rate times and, for some houses, party lines with the family next door. There wasn't any choice. And why did somebody choose 999 as the emergency number when it clearly took the longest possible time to dial? Surely, 111 would have been quicker and might have saved vital seconds in a life-or-death situation. Then the trimphone came along – you know, the one Noel Edmonds favoured on *Swap Shop* – which even came in a fake wood trim. Compared to the old-style phone – and the first mobiles – it was also virtually weightless. So much so that as soon as you started dialling, the whole thing would fall off the table.

I know I'm not alone in seeing the mobile as a necessary

evil. Brilliant for sorting out childcare arrangements, calling out the lifeboat, all that kind of stuff, but I think we're all aware of the downsides. Ringtones are a particular *bête noire*, especially that little *bête verte*, the Crazy Frog, one species I would personally be happy to see hunted to extinction. And I'd prefer it if nobody ever texted me. The screen's too small, and my fingers are too big to reply. I may be entering the prime of life, but I would still rather have to leave the specs neatly tucked out of sight. Texting: we spend thousands of years perfecting language and now we're back with hieroglyphs – ☹.

Real life or Second Life

Sim city

11 November 1983 Hitchhiker's Guide to the Galaxy *author Douglas Adams and* Spitting Image *producer John Lloyd publish* The Meaning of Liff.

I can't work out where these people find the time. I have difficulty fitting in the most basic demands of life in the twenty-first century, along with being a parent, husband and diligent son and son-in-law, let alone the really important jobs like removing the crap the kids have left in the back of the car every week, or allocating several days to watch the latest Nadal/Federer marathon. And I've still got a to-do list stretching off into the far distance.

So who the hell has the time to become a resident of Second Life? The Second Life slogan is 'Your world. Your imagination'. And one is naturally tempted to add 'You're full of shite.'

The fans say it allows them to be whoever they want to be – but that's exactly the same argument its detractors use. First, because finding out who you *actually* are is a key part of being a grown-up. And second, because when you shimmy up to some foxy brunette in a Second Life nightclub, the buffed body, chiselled look and dubious name (Donkey John) you've handpicked for your personal avatar belie the fact that in actuality your paunch is hanging over the elasticated waistband of the same trackie bottoms you've been wearing since last week. Likewise, the brunette propping up the bar is more than likely a pimply teen geek from Swindon.

The nearest equivalent to this in the 1970s, I guess, was citizens' band radio. The CB craze had a lot of the same characteristics – horny call signs which redneck truckers and toothless waitresses could hide behind. I really would rather have a stab at the real-life thing, despite all the stress it involves.

And besides, if I ever want to spend time with the Sim(m)s, I'll get in touch with my friend John.

Randy Andy or Harry

Royal princes

19 November 1983 David Frost interviews Prince Andrew on TV-am in the year Andrew split with Koo Stark, after returning from seeing action as a navy pilot in the Falklands.

Every generation of the royal family should have one black sheep, one maverick prince or princess to highlight the devotion to duty of the rellies – a Duke of Windsor, charming, fey, reckless, exiled to Paris, standing in contrast to his brother King George VI, shy, dedicated, loyal. For the Queen's generation, it was her sister Margaret Rose, lounging in huge shades and a kaftan in the shadows of her villa on Mustique, with Roddy 'the gardener' Llewellyn paying court.

So it was a little worrying when the Queen's older children showed signs of all being really quite sensible – Anne picking up the BBC Sports Personality of the Year award for her equestrian skills, Charles being solemnly invested as Prince of Wales, tootling off to Cambridge, eventually getting married and producing two male heirs to offset any concerns about the succession.

It was a huge relief, then, when their younger brother rose to the challenge. Randy Andy, the playboy prince, squired the likes of cheeky Koo Stark around town and popped on his flying helmet to nip down to the Falklands. Then he found himself a flame-haired bride and set up home in glorious *Dallas*-style extravagance at Southyork. Hurrah, a royal prince with shit taste, as was most emphatically demonstrated when he hooked up with his brother Edward, the aforementioned redheaded Princess and various other royals to launch *It's a Royal Knockout* on an unsuspecting nation. It was Live Aid for Sloane Rangers and Hooray Henrys with shields and lances.

As Andrew mellowed, and seemed to disappear completely from sight, the torch of blacksheepery was handed on to the next generation. Prince Harry took his uncle as a role model – active service in a war zone, a penchant for clubbing and sexy companions – and added his own twists, especially the total suspension of thought when faced with the racks of outfits on display in the Chippenham branch of Fancy-Dress Clothes R Us. The lad shows great promise, and I look forward to seeing how he will develop the role. A couple of illegitimate kids and marriage to a lap-dancer would keep us all interested and watching the Queen's speech. 'My bastard great-grand-children and I . . .'

Filofax or Palm Pilot

Time management

1 January 1984 The first entry in the new Filofax diary – 1984 is the classic year for the Filofax as a yuppie accessory, more than sixty years after the organiser was first launched.

I'm not a Palm Pilot person. And blackberries should be confined to smoothies or crumbles. But I do still have a Filofax. I never used a diary, even as a kid, though each Christmas one of those tiny ones with a pencil in the spine, usually a Scouts one, would be tucked into the old sock at the end of the bed. Dateline 1973: a ten-year-old boy's entry for a typical day at home would have been along the lines of: 'Got up. Kicked a ball against a wall for ten hours. Watched *Screentest*. Had dinner. Went to bed.' Date line 2008: 'Up at crack of dawn, dropped off by mum and Neville at dad's, 'cos it's his weekend to have me. Judo, family therapy session, SATs cramming class, tennis. Played PSX for ten hours, didn't go to bed.'

But I fell for the Filofax, and I have no real idea why – maybe I thought my life would be miraculously transformed if it was neatly divided into tabbed sections. The Filofax was like a pochette (the male purse that French gents sported) crammed with useless information.

Cheese and winetasting notes at five quid a pop. Fantastic. Can't find a side-street in Prague? I'm your man.

Barbie or Bratz

Girly stuff

9 March 1984 Barbie celebrates her official twenty-fifth birthday with a gala party in New York, with Andy Warhol on the guest list, and a Peaches n' cream outfit to follow 1983's aerobics Great Shape Barbie look.

You'll have to forgive me. I'm one of two brothers, so I never got to play with anything other than toys for boys. So I have taken advice from my consultant on all girly stuff, my wife. Here's her list of essential nostalgia for girls:

- Roller skates – bit gay for boys
- My Little Pony – of course
- *Girl's World* magazine along with *Jackie* and *Fab 208* – there was also a *Girl's World* head you could practise hair and make-up on
- Barbie versus Sindy – like Tommy Gunn against Action Man, Sindy was Britain's plucky pretender to an American invader
- Making 'perfume' by stuffing rose petals and blossom in water
- Kaleidoscopes
- Tiny Tears dolls

Thing's Ain't What They Used to Be

- Sticklebricks
- 'Clapping' games
- Mixing blackcurrant cordial with milk
- And, my favourite, because I had absolutely no idea what they are – Wade Whimsies, little collectible china animals. Bless.

Kissogram or lapdancer

Stag nights

29 June 1984 Tom Hanks stars in *Bachelor Party*, a template for all future stag nights: 'Let's have a bachelor party with chicks and guns and fire trucks and hookers and drugs and booze!'

Stag nights used to be simple affairs. The best man would round up a few of the groom's mates, suggest a time to meet in the Black Horse the night before the great day, and then all concerned would try to down as many pints as possible along the High Street before closing time, while winding up the husband-to-be about the doom that awaited him. The worst that could happen was that the lads would strip the groom and send him up on the milk train to Crewe with only a Red Star parcel sticker to protect his wedding tackle.

The mid-'80s invention of the kissogram changed the mood, as the groom – previously only worried about how he would get back from Cheshire in time for the ceremony – had the ominous prospect hanging over the entire evening of a buxom policewoman bursting into the bar and delivering a doggerel poem followed by a smacker on the lips or, worse, popping a ghetto blaster on the floor and proceeding to force the hapless soul into unhooking her bra.

Stag nights are now big business. The best man sends out an itinerary six months ahead of time, with details of the visas, injections, bank loans and time off required. The logistics are military in scale, with the hiring of an entire lapdancing club in Vilnius usually part of the upfront costs demanded from every participant. But after all the preparations and all the investment, the night still boils down to the groom and a dozen mates drinking themselves stupid – only now *everybody* has to work out how the hell they're going to get home in one piece.

Cash or plastic

Money, money, money

22 July 1984 Seve Ballesteros wins the Open Championship at St Andrew's, his second Open and fourth major, giving him the kind of fame that makes him an ideal face for American Express: 'Don't leave home without it.'

Very occasionally, you'll bump into some obstreperous codger who never left the pre-decimal era. 'That'll be two bob in old money.' The names of the old coins had a great Dickensian chink to them – guineas, florins, half crowns, two-bob bits and tanners. *Blue Peter* held a competition to come up with nicknames for the new coins, but none ever stuck.

The most obvious downside of the old system was the maths involved. For any generally innumerate schoolkid it was a bloody relief to put an end to dividing £1 17s 6d by five and swap over to the far easier decimal sums. And, as time has gone, our trouser pockets have felt the relief of not carting around tonnes of metal. That's good. As is the ability to get cash out when you need it – until the mid-'70s, when the banks shut on Friday afternoon, that was it until Monday. No cash, unless you pawned the pet. For us kids, money was all about Post Office savings books, paying everything out in 5ps from our pocket money, and postal orders for Christmas.

But although spending money is lighter, faster and it's smarter to zip everything through a magnetic strip or a chip, there's no tactile sense of just how much you're spending. Two quid at the corner shop, Switch it. Five thousand quid at the Harrod's sale, Switch it. And by the time some bastard's hacked into your online bank details, and you've been scammed and skimmed, your identity cloned and your credit drained dry, the old codger with his sock under the mattress full of cash – even if most of it is in one-pound notes, threepenny bits and halfpennies – is looking mighty smug.

Old Spice or Jean-Paul Gaultier

Aftershaves

17 November 1984 'Our 'Enry', boxing hero Henry Cooper, makes a cameo appearance on the *Cannon and Ball Show* – after retiring from the ring he was known as the 'splash it all over' face of Brut.

There he was, Peter Wyngarde, the man we knew better as Jason King from *Department S*, a swashbuckling dandy for the 1970s, sauntering – positively swaggering – across the TV screen during a commercial break. Cue the voice-over: 'Peter Wyngarde smells . . .' There was a slight crunch of gravel as Wyngarde stopped mid-stride. He turned, looked straight at the camera and raised a haughty eyebrow, until the voice-over continued, 'great!' The stern look relaxed, as he smiled and smugly continued on his way, leaving behind, we imagined, a whiff of the aftershave in question. Wonderful – a subtle and self-deprecating dig at the Jason King character. It was probably *too good* a performance, because everyone was so focused on Wyngarde that nobody seems to remember what the cologne was.

The advertising business spent quite a lot of that period persuading red-blooded men that wearing aftershave would not in any way dilute their manliness. That's why they had to wheel on Henry Cooper, 'Our 'Enry', to splash Brut all over himself. You couldn't question the virility of a geezer who'd had the temerity to dump Cassius Clay on his rear end. Henry was kosher, and if the great smell of Brut was good enough for his burly frame, then it was good enough for any dad's stocking filler. But if Brut didn't take his fancy there was always the salty tang of Old Spice, or, for the racier gent, a dash of Blue Stratos or Denim.

Spattered with these exotic lotions, the sweet-smelling '70s bloke could dream of encountering a woman who bathed in Badedas. One dunk in this chestnut-flavoured bath foam would apparently send her into a highly pitched state of arousal, and she'd post herself, clad only in a silk dressing-gown, half hidden behind the curtain of a suite in a country hotel, waiting for the arrival of the cologne-doused stud who'd screech up in his convertible Jag. This fantasy was far-fetched, especially for a teenager from north London who was still trying to use up his Matey bubble bath from last Christmas, and just as remote as the possibility of meeting the girl who wrapped her lips around a Cadbury's Flake in slow motion. If you ever did hook up with a girl who was that fond of Flakes, chances were that she liked them so much she was about to sign up for Weight Watchers.

As the male cologne market expanded, Old Spice and Brut were left behind, with just a faint hint of those stalwarts drifting on the winds of change. Of all the new aftershaves (and even the deodorants that promised to get you some action) the most outrageous has to be the scent created by Jean-Paul Gaultier, the impish French fashion guru who popped up on *Eurotrash*, and his little matelot bottle of smelly stuff. Even with the best will in the world, it was hard to imagine Jean-Paul going twelve rounds with 'Our 'Enry'.

Sinclair C5 or MacAir

Tomorrow's World

10 January 1985 Sir Clive Sinclair launches his battery-powered C5, one of the more spectacular product flops of the last century.

Here we are, living in Tomorrow's World, and inevitably it's some way from the vision of the future that Raymond Baxter and his team predicted on the TV show (another classic theme tune, this time courtesy of John Dankworth). Raymond, his wartime RAF fighter-pilot credentials giving him a certain level of authority, presented an array of inventions that often looked as if they had been dreamed up by the *Blue Peter* presenters, but the prospect of the work-free, leisure-rich lifestyle they sketched out was appealing. In the years after man had landed on the moon, we were all aspiring astronauts at heart, so it seemed perfectly reasonable to assume that by 2008 we would all be dining on small round pills and drinks from vacuum packs that contained all our dietary requirements – while all visiting Martians would be happily tucking into giant bowls of Smash. And you *can* live that dream, so long as you're happy to subsist on a diet of Smarties, vitamin supplements and Sports Lucozade, and I dare say some people do – supermodels, perhaps.

It was no surprise to see the great James Burke, one of

Raymond's eager assistants (others included Bob Symes, William Woollard, Judith Hann and Kieran Prendeville), fronting the BBC coverage of the Apollo missions, clambering in and out of mock-ups of the latest lunar module. Those were dramatic times. Live feeds were beamed into our homes from the Kennedy Space Center, which had received them directly from the crews' quarters on board the rockets. These images were always edgy and unpredictable, none more so than those from *Apollo 13*, when everyone waited with baited breath to see if the astronauts would make it back home. It was one of those genuine global events when satellite broadcasting could create an instant, simultaneous worldwide audience for an unfolding drama, just as happened with the Munich Olympics hostage crisis in 1972.

We are getting almost blasé about the constant flood of technological product launches these days. Every year, every month, every week, there are phenomenal leaps forward in miniaturisation, memory power, connectivity. This means the manufacturers can encourage us to bin last year's iPod or wafer-thin MacAir laptop because they are already dated, but the new releases come so thick and fast that it's a blur. During the '70s, although the groundwork for the digital revolution was being laid somewhere deep in Silicon Valley, the launch of a new invention was still a major event. The essential design of the car hadn't changed since the early part of the century, the TV was still a cathode-ray tube, as it had been in John Logie Baird's day (colour was the big breakthrough, arriving in 1968), and radio was still mostly broadcast on medium wave.

There were refinements and new models but rarely anything revolutionary. When the early computers appeared they required vast amounts of ticker tape, and calculators were the size of the Isle of Man.

Gradually, though, the pace picked up. Videotape had a huge impact, so long as you didn't plump for a Betamax machine. (Pub bores still insist that Betamax was a better system than VHS, while true aficionados continue to hanker after the Philips/Grundig Video 2000, which they claim was superior to both. Sorry, I'm losing the will to live myself here.) The Walkman was undoubtedly a revolution in the way we listened to music. Early mobile phones and faxes were the first signs of a tidal wave of change. In the summer of 1983 home computers broke big with Alan Sugar's Amstrad, the Commodore 64 and the Sinclair Spectrum all vying for the market lead. The software was supplied on cassettes that took half an hour to load, with crazy lines flicking across the screen of the Sony Trinitron, just so you could play Pacman.

And then there was the Sinclair C5. There was a huge fanfare about Sir Clive Sinclair's personal, battery-powered transporter. We were told it would change commuting habits for ever. But after a massive unveiling there was only a stunned silence followed by the sound of sniggering kids ridiculing anyone brave enough to tootle past them on one. All they saw was a little white sidecar lacking one vital ingredient, the motorbike to go with it, like Gromit detached from Wallace in *A Close Shave*. This was the stuff of cartoon comedy. And probably the last completely crap invention of the '80s.

Miami Vice or *CSI: Miami*

Cop shows

26 February 1985 The first screening on British TV of *Miami Vice*, the hot new cop show that had premiered on NBC the previous autumn.

One of my earliest TV roles was about six lines playing a git in *The Bill*.

It felt like a tenuous toehold in the great and long tradition of TV cop shows. Early memories are filled with the no-nonsense British coppers of *Z Cars* and *Softly Softly* (incidentally, my father's first directing credentials were on both series) in which Stratford Johns was a solid, stolid slab of unflappable British common sense, and where every officer knew his duty – 'to uphold the law, ma'am' – and his place in the hierarchy of the police station, as though the inmates of Stalag Luft III had moved straight from demob into the British police force *en masse*. The programmes were set in tough northern cities (*Z Cars* in 'Newtown' on Merseyside), Lowry paintings brought to life, and the overriding mood was realism.

That's why the arrival on TV of the American imports was such a jolt to the system, albeit a pleasant one. Paul Michael Glaser's Starsky and David Soul's Hutch maintaining law and order on the streets of LA (rather than

Hartley) brought a shaft of Californian sunshine and glamour to the proceedings. For most of us, America still seemed a very long way away. And the pair not only had plenty of banter but *that* car and the driving techniques. The car, a red two-door Ford Torino with a white stripe down the side, was key. Starsky driving slowly with the door open while Hutch walked alongside, gun pulled, was a classic manoeuvre. In *Life on Mars*, every time Hunt, Sam Tyler, Raymondo and Chris got in or out of Gene's Ford, we made sure to shut all the doors exactly in sync. Simm's idea and our little homage to *Starsky and Hutch*.

That period of US cop shows was full of sharply observed characters, from Colombo to Ironside, and great support actors. Telly Savalas's Kojak would not have been the same without his support team, Captain Frank McNeil, Crocker, Stavros, Saperstein and Rizzo. That show also prepared a nation for their first flights to New York on Freddie Laker's Skytrain – because the Big Apple was *exactly* like it looked on *Kojak*, with steam emerging from street grilles, and everyone carrying deli takeaways of pastrami on rye in brown paper bags.

By the middle of the next decade, the location scouts were on the lookout for new settings, and the choice of Florida for *Miami Vice* was inspired. This was the perfect '80s city – luminous colours, Ferraris, speedboats, an MTV soundtrack, pastel fashions, ridiculous amounts of coke. Crockett and Tubbs' boss, Lieutenant Castillo, worked in an office made out of glass bricks housing a single designer desk and nothing else. For fook's sake!

The counterbalance to all that would be provided by

British TV. The psychological shows of the '90s like *Cracker* and *Prime Suspect* kept the realism but added a fresh twist. The genre was so established by then that it could be parodied – in *The Thin Blue Line*: *Z Cars* meets *Some Mothers Do 'Ave 'Em* – or given the nostalgia treatment in *Midsomer Murders* and *Morse*, both nods to an earlier time of cogitation and deduction. As was . . . well, you can guess which show I'm thinking of now. Perhaps that's why I haven't been grabbed by the new wave of US shows like *CSI: Miami*.

Although it was never a cop show, I must put in a short plug here for *Mission: Impossible*, a groundbreaking thriller series, so crisp, so beautifully constructed, so gripping, that when the immaculate *Persuaders* was put up against it on American TV it never took off, even with Roger Moore and Tony Curtis onboard.

Which tenuous link leads me to a story involving a fantastic director's note to an actor. It was from *State of Play*, directed by David Yates, who also went on to direct the later Harry Potter movies. In one scene, an actress had to walk towards the camera for about twenty-five seconds. Count that in your head and, believe you me, that's quite a long time to be walking on your own. Just you. Well, there's walking and there's walking, and the scene wasn't happening to David's or the actress's liking. So he simply told her to play the theme tune of *Mission Impossible* in her head as she walked. Instant wrap.

Slide rule or Excel

Maths

4 July 1985 Ruth Lawrence is awarded a starred first in maths at Oxford University, aged thirteen, becoming the youngest British person to receive a first-class degree.

I was never good at maths. And I'm frankly bamboozled whenever financial advisers start flashing up their Excel spreadsheets. You can carbon-date the level of maths I reached before losing the plot, because my idea of advanced calculating equipment is the slide rule, which was presumably relegated to dinosaur status *circa* 1973 by the arrival of even the most elementary of electronic calculators. But I have fond memories of the slide rule (which proved handy for dissecting flies, even though I had absolutely no idea what it was really meant to do). It's an essential part of any maths kit, along with a pair of compasses (handy for amateur tattooing if used in combination with a leaky fountain pen), and a combination plastic protractor and set square. You'll be pleased to know that there are a few slide rule websites – Eric's Slide Rule Site will give you all the background you could ever need. Eric recently announced with pride that he has greatly expanded the Cleaning Your Slide Rule section. Nice one, Eric.

Live Aid or Live 8

Charidee gigs

13 July 1985 At midday, Live Aid kicks off at Wembley Stadium. Following the Coldstream Guards' fanfare and the National Anthem, Status Quo launch into 'Rockin' All Over the World'.

I was nine months old when JFK was downed in Dealey Plaza and only six when *Apollo 11* landed on the moon. But there are later events that can instantly transport me back in time. John Lennon being shot. Charles and Di getting spliced. And, of course, Live Aid. The first – and probably the best – great worldwide charity event, the self-proclaimed 'global jukebox'.

On that beautiful July Saturday in 1985 I was twenty-two. My parents had gone out for the day so I invited a bunch of chums over to make a party of it. This was going to be a big event – everybody knew it. We'd all picked up the buzz from the Band Aid single the Christmas before, had enjoyed watching the video of the recording session, with the Status Quo lads having such a good time. Maybe they misunderstood Bob and Midge when they declared everybody was going to have a line . . .

And now here we were, round the screen, midday, and there were Francis Rossi and Rick Parfitt giving the whole event the best possible start. Later there was a list of acts to savour, from Sade to U2 to Queen. Phil Collins was going to play at Wembley, then jump on Concorde and perform at JFK in Philadelphia too – nobody knew what a carbon footprint was back then. St Bob was telling the audience to 'Give us the money *now*', and the hapless presenter to 'Fuck the address, let's get the phone numbers.'

Ever since we haven't been able to move for charidee. Telethons, gigs, or dodging the charity hustlers on the High Street, smiling pathetically at the *Big Issue* seller. Maybe I'm too cynical, but however worthy, I can't help thinking that maybe it's an easy way to offload responsibility from government on to the rest of us . . . And in any case, there are just way too many people bombarding us with requests. The big stadium shows have lost the power they once had. They'll never match the impact of Live Aid. Look at Live 8: lovely to see the Floyd back together again, but Pete Doherty should have spent time studying old footage of Jimmy Page to see how to perform magnificently when completely wasted.

Old Labour or New Labour

Socialism

1 October 1985 Neil Kinnock gets a standing ovation at the Labour Party Conference in Bournemouth as he takes on Militant and Arthur Scargill to reunite a shattered party.

During the power cuts of the Heath government, the whole nation sat huddled round the weak glow of a candle, with nothing to do but watch the luminous hands of a Timex watch circle round – no Nintendo DS to keep us amused. Those blackouts were the closest we kids got to a glimpse of what life in the Blitz must have been like.

Mums up and down the land had stomped around muttering about 'Margaret Thatcher, milk snatcher', when the Education Minister cut free school milk in 1971. (I can definitely remember the time before that when the little crates of miniature milk bottles would be delivered to our primary school. On cold winter days, by the time the crates were brought in the milk would have frozen and the silver tops would be perched on top of little columns of watery ice-cream.)

By 1979, when Thatcher was voted in as PM, it almost seemed a relief, because the final days of the Wilson/Callaghan era had been so dark. Sunny Jim Callaghan's jovial denial of any chaos when he flew home in January from a summit in Guadeloupe led to the *Sun*'s famous 'Crisis? What Crisis?' headline. The subs were obviously big Supertramp fans back then – little could they guess that the *Crime of the Century* was about to follow. So Mrs T cruised into Number 10 but soon she started struggling too. Luckily for her, though, Labour self-destructed as the Limehouse Four set up the SDP with that exquisitely, excruciatingly early '80s logo, all primary colours, the party pitching itself like a groovy ad agency.

Then the Falklands rescued Thatcherism from almost certain defeat. It still seems extraordinary that we made such a fuss about it. If the Argentinians had occupied the Shetlands or the Isle of Wight for the last hundred years, surely we would have thought *that* was out of order. But it seemed the majority had sided with Thatcher and Murdoch. The task force was dispatched with balloons and bunting for a five-week cruise around the globe, giving the Argies plenty of warning that we were on our way – and they still weren't ready.

I think they missed a trick. Argentina should have hung on for another twenty-six years and invaded in 2008. With every man jack of the tattered remains of the British armed forces stretched to breaking point in Kabul and Basra, they'd have been able to breeze in to Port Stanley. The only task force we'd have been able to send down to the South Atlantic would have been the *Ground Force* team: Titchmarsh, Dimmock and that bloke with the toolbelt hiding out of sight behind a freshly painted picket fence. For air cover, maybe Stelios in an Easyjet, although with the hike in fuel prices he'd have only made it to the

Algarve. And from the sea, Cracknell and Fogle in their rowing boat, with an estimated arrival time of spring 2020.

As it was, Thatcher won, and cemented her position. Michael Foot, that splendid, inspiring debater in the Commons, was brushed aside in 1983, a don in a donkey jacket, brilliant but not a party leader, defiantly keeping the faith as the election results deluged him. Then Neil Kinnock started the process of reinventing the Labour Party, pilloried by the Tory press, mercilessly crucified, a decent man who, since resigning the leadership after John Major blagged the 1992 election, has retained his dignity.

I loved all those south Wales politicians, their oratory, their passion, but Neil made two crucial mistakes. Waving to the press on Brighton beach and giving them a perfect pratfall. And then that overly triumphant speech just before the '92 vote: 'Well, alrrright!' 'Stop, Neil.' But on and on he went, and the damage was done.

No more Welsh firebrands, and the Tartan Army took over: the late John Smith, Tony B (Fettes School Scottish) and Gordon B. Suddenly the cabinet was as Scottish as a kilted haggis on Burns Night.

Personally, I think Tony Blair should have embraced all the accusations of cronyism and brought in a whole kitchen cabinet of the extended Clan Blair. Alongside Met Commissioner Sir Ian Blair, he could have found positions for Lionel, Linda and the lovely Isla.

Blue Nun or Fat Bastard

In vino veritas

21 November 1985 French law specifies the third Thursday in every November as the launch of each year's new Beaujolais, and the 'Beaujolais nouveau' marketing campaign goes into overdrive.

It was one of the highlights of each autumn in the 1980s. Beaujolais nouveau. A wine-fuelled *Wacky Races* as vintage carloads of toffs in blazers and bow ties thundered through the byways of northern France, desperate to deliver crates of the stuff to Peter Dominic's. Terrific fun, chaps. Only the whole hoohah was a huge scam, the wine so immature it was still in nappies, and the French wine-growers cockahoop that they'd found a market dumb enough to dump it on. While we gaily cried, *'Le Beaujolais nouveau est arrivé!'*, a grinning posse of Gallic *viniculteurs* chorused back, *'Les nincompoops britanniques sont complète-ment cons!'* We were *completèment* conned, that's for sure.

This merely went to prove that, as a nation, outside a small circle of connoisseurs and sellers, we knew diddly squat about wine.

Back in the '70s there wasn't much to choose from. Paul Masson from California in the carafe that could always double later as a flower vase. Chianti, the bottle again granted an afterlife, caked with candlewax and in its nifty wicker basket to provide that *Lady and the Tramp* trattoria vibe for a late-night seduction. And Mateus Rosé. Along with Piat d'Or, that was pretty much the range on offer if you weren't frequenting the specialist wine merchants in St James's.

The globalisation of brands has meant that even the local 7-Eleven now sells wine from every corner of the world. Very convenient, but any sense of adventure has disappeared. And it's the same with beer. It used to be the only place you could enjoy a San Miguel was on holiday in Spain, or a Peroni on a long weekend in Rome. Now even the most obscure ale from the micro-breweries of the Midwest, or Brazil's fourth-favourite lager, is on the shelves at Asda.

To stand out from the crowd, the dumb-arse wine names arrived. Suppose they amused the lads on the City trading desks. 'Rupert, I've just sent a bottle of Fat Bastard to Julian in hedge funds . . . 'cos he's a fat bastard. *Seriously* bloody funny.'

Six of the best or an ASBO

'This will hurt me more than it hurts you'

22 July 1986 Parliament votes by the narrowest of margins (231–230) to ban the cane and the slipper from state schools. It was another twenty-two years before all schools were included in the ban.

Ah yes, the gentle art of discipline. When I was at school discipline was delivered in the shape of a slipper. And by slipper, I don't mean the kind of cosy, tweedy footwear your grandad popped on of an evening. No, the slipper in question was a high-calibre variant on the black PE plimsoll, with a suitably flesh-coloured sole and a whippy flexibility guaranteed to inflict a stinging aftershock and some attractive indentations on your palm. (The marks were vital for impressing your friends and proving you'd taken your punishment with nary a whimper.)

The first time I encountered the slipper was after I'd been dispatched to the headmaster for a minor infringement, answering back in class or something equally footling. Off I trotted, and after shuffling uneasily for a while on a chair outside his office I was summoned inside, my misdemeanour was gravely discussed, and the slipper sentence was pronounced. Now, here's the weird thing. I knew I was going to get the requisite three thwacks, but

---

even so I instinctively pulled my hand away when the first blow fell, like some kind of practical joke. But there was no hiding-place. Thereafter the blows fell sure and sweet, the black art handed down from headmaster to headmaster since Tom Brown's schooldays.

That was the official punishment, but most teachers were more free-form. Some possessed an uncanny ability to throw a piece of chalk over their shoulder, without turning round, and hit a chatterer or general smart-arse in the temple with unerring accuracy.

Once, during woodwork (does that still even exist? If it does, it's probably called ligneous design technology now). I was working on a coffee table, patiently planing it down from a large slab of teak. This should have been second nature, since my grandfather Sidney was a handicraft teacher specialising in woodwork, but I was certainly no chip off the old block. Unfortunately, I'd taken one too many chips off this particular block, and ended up with a shapeless object more like a clog than a table.

I was slaving over my masterpiece and not concentrating fully on an explanation of the niceties of the mortise and tenon joint, when – *Wallop!* – a large chunk of wood was dispatched and landed on the back of my head. Deeply unfair, I thought, and now I'd have been radioing in the litigation squad immediately. Then I shrugged it off and got back to planing my piece of teak – and ended up with a coffee table that Barbie would have been proud of.

Step out of line today and there won't be any clip round the ear. Pupils' rights rule – one thwack and any teacher would instantly find themselves in a YouTube clip and out on their ear. Discipline has been offloaded to the coppers, which is surely a victory for the ASBO generation and an admission that – as any fule kno – respect for teachers has gone, along with an errant piece of chalk, out of the window.

Yuppies or dotcommers

Rich kids

27 October 1986 'Big Bang', the deregulation of the Stock Exchange, a cornerstone of Thatcherite policies, is a landmark date in the rise of the yuppie.

When Judgement Day comes round, and all the old yuppies are rounded up and taken away, I'll be waving them farewell. I can be accused of many social failings, I'm sure, but on that one I have a clean licence. I never signed up to the Thatcherite vision. I'd have been useless as a yuppie, anyway. I'm not big on red-rimmed glasses or braces and I don't like spritzers – that's just watering down wine, you wimps, and then, to compound the sin, sticking in ice cubes. A shocking lapse of taste. And what a load of ponce cocktails are. Now a dry Martini is perfect, especially if the vermouth barely grazes the gin. But all that Tom Cruise bollocks, no.

The fallout's still with us. We did some filming for *Ashes to Ashes* in Canary Wharf one weekend. The place was deserted, very odd indeed, an absolute ghost town, like something out of *Logan's Run*. And the whole property ladder dream really started in the 1980s, so it's the yuppies' fault that we now have to suffer all those endless property and relocation shows and broom cupboards in Kensington on sale for half a million.

Worse, the yuppies morphed into dotcommers and hedge-fund managers (and what do they do, exactly?). That's where the real money is. An elderly friend went on a cruise recently and was surprised to see a couple of women in their early twenties relaxing on deck among all the retirees. 'What are you doing on a cruise?' he asked, imagining they'd prefer a Club 18–30 holiday. 'Oh,' they said breezily, 'we just sold our dotcom business for a gazillion dollars so we've retired.'

The thing about dotcom geeks is that those kids you used to sneer at in the playground because they stayed behind after school for extra Science Club and played with soldering irons have taken over the planet. We used to dream of being rock stars because they had unimaginable wealth and private jets (think Led Zep's Starship), but the music business boys are paupers in comparison. Sell a dotcom, buy a small Latin American country.

Bungee jumps or tombstoning

Extreme sports

13 November 1986 Hod-carrier Michael Lush is killed in rehearsal for an item on Noel Edmonds' *Late Late Breakfast Show*, a stunt that required him to bungee jump from a 120-foot crane. The series is cancelled two days later.

This is the subject where, sadly, I kiss goodbye to any hope of a hard-man image. I have never once jumped out of a plane and entrusted my life to a large silk handkerchief and a few bits of string. Likewise, I've never been tempted to hurtle to certain death protected only by a large elastic band. Tombstoning – jumping off a cliff or a pier into a few inches of water? No, thanks – the name is a bit of a give-away.

I'm not a complete wuss, though, I'd like to point out. I used to be a talented hedgehopper, an early version of free running. A simple, but brilliant, sport that involved running towards and jumping on to the top of a bush – a rhododendron ideally; they were the best. In general I leave the dangerous sports to the professionals, like Evel Knievel – remember those wind-up Evel Knievel Dare Devil stunt sets with the bike that did all the flips and wheelies and jumped through a blazing ring of fire (i.e. a ring of cardboard)?

Evel was the man, Elvis on two wheels – the '68 Comeback Elvis, not the bloated hamburger-munching one. It was such big news when Evel came over to Wembley Stadium to jump a dozen or so buses. In one camera shot from inside the players' tunnel, Evel screeched into the entrance and the cameraman lurched left, but only at the very last minute. The best thing about Evel was that he always crashed. He was obviously winging those stunts at Caesar's Palace and the Snake River Canyon, and clearly had no idea whether he was going to succeed. *Blam!* He'd crash. Again. Managed to escape with a few broken vertebrae, then jump again. Real bottle and great entertainment.

Those '70s stuntmen were true nutters at a time when the most dangerous thing kids could do was play with a pair of Klackers (a.k.a. Ker-knockers), those dangling balls which all schools immediately outlawed, claiming that the balls could shatter into a hail of shrapnel. No, they just couldn't bear the incessant click-clacking. Evel, Eddie Kidd – our homegrown version – and Karl Wallenda, the guy who fell to his death in 1978 when attempting a tightrope walk (at the age of seventy-three!) between two skyscrapers in Puerto Rico, and inadvertently provided a horribly gripping piece of TV.

We had a great stunt co-ordinator on *Life on Mars*, Peter Brayham, who died not long after and is much missed. Peter always doubled for John Wayne, and could win any stunt-related argument with the killer line, 'Well, as I told the Duke . . .'

Ollie Reed or Lily Allen

Raising hell

21 February 1987 At a recording of *Aspel & Company*, Oliver Reed runs amok and entertains the nation with a famously drunken rendition of 'The Wild One', regularly voted one of TV's top moments.

If you were a chat-show host in the 1980s one sure-fire way to liven things up was to invite Oliver Reed along as a guest. Invariably he'd emerge after some considerable length of time in the green room, tanked up and raring to go. He did his party piece for Michael Aspel several times, for Des O'Connor and later on *The Word*. And he asked Richard Madeley why he was orange. Clive James was a fellow guest on the infamous 1987 outing, and asked a seriously drunk Ollie why he drank. 'The finest people', he replied majestically, if waveringly, 'I have ever met in my life are in pubs.'

He was part of a celebrated quartet of acting roister-doisterers, along with Richard Burton, Richard Harris and Peter O'Toole. Their benders were legendary. Lost weekends spent downing crates of Guinness, wine, Scotch, vodka, gin and crème de menthe, topped off by Reed in one session with 'a bottle of Babycham'. There's a story about Ollie turning up for a christening where he was godfather – the perfect guardian of the little one's morals. He was drunk, needless to say, but then so were the baby's parents, the godmother *and* the vicar. Up went the cry from a pew towards the back of the church, 'All we need is a slice of lemon in the font.'

Like all drunks, these hellraisers were capable of being bores, boars and boors when trashed. But they were Technicolor widescreen characters, larger than life, and their livers larger than Hampshire.

In the hellraiser heyday there was a tacit agreement with the Lunchtime O'Boozes of the press to keep things under wraps. That's not possible any more. Have a half of shandy too many and there'll be somebody with a mobile filming your indiscretions, and beaming it to NewsCorp within seconds. Or a young starlet's PR rep will discreetly let it be known that his client will be falling out of Bouji's around 4 a.m., and might just be going commando. So if Lily Allen enjoys a lively night out, she gets tagged as the descendant of Reed, Burton and co., which she clearly isn't. After all, who in their twenties hasn't staggered out of a club in the wee small hours – it'd be stranger if she hadn't.

A little actor's insight. The lager or bitter in pub scenes is always non-alcoholic. It used to be cold tea. The trick, for any actor who couldn't face that, was always to ask for a Guinness, because the props boys can't fake a Guinness.

Irish coffee or tall wet skinny cappuccino
Sophisticated brews

15 August 1987 Former Starbucks employee Howard Schultz acquires the company, consisting at the time of just six outlets in the Seattle metropolitan area.

Why do we have to make everything so complicated? Coffee is a simple drink. Coffee granules, boiling water, and milk, result: a cup of coffee to kickstart the morning. The granules could have been Nescafé Gold Blend, and Gareth Hunt and his shaking coffee beans probably reminded you to stick a jar in the shopping trolley. But that was all. If you wanted more sophistication, it was simply a matter of nipping to the local Beefeater, ordering an Irish coffee, and luxuriating with that funny, curvy, glass-handled jug with some artery-clogging cream floating on the top and a hit of whisky to make it a bit cheeky – then everybody drove home. Not sophisticated enough? Try the Kahlúa option for a Mexican coffee, or Tia Maria for a Calypso coffee. For extra exoticism, the '80s saw the return of '50s-style hubble-bubbling espresso machines – remember the ad for instant coffee where the hostess made the gurgling noise in the kitchen to convince the guests she'd freshly brewed the coffee?

But we couldn't leave it at that, could we? I can now

spend half an hour in the queue at Starbucks or Costa Coffee waiting for someone further up the line to work their way through the infinite options on offer. By the time they've decided that this morning it's going to be a venti skinny decaf frozen macchiato with soy cream and a dusting of nougat, I've usually lost the will to live.

Local boozer or gastropub

Hurry up, Harry, come on/We're all goin' down the pub

19 May 1988 The new Liquor Licensing Act comes into force and means that pubs in England and Wales can now legally serve alcohol all afternoon.

At heart, the pub experience is a recognisable descendant of the way things were. You go to the bar, order a round, sit down, finish your drink, go back to the bar, order another round, *ad nauseam* (literally, if you develop a taste for the liqueurs on the top shelf).

Now, though, there are fewer pubs. It's depressing to see how many corner pubs have been decommissioned and converted into flats or takeaways – and of the ones that remain an alarmingly high percentage have been subsumed into the chains of the Ferret, Frog, Flamingo, Friggit and Firkin variety, though I suppose at least that keeps them open and trading.

There is also no fug. The toxic cloud that hovered in every bar, hanging permanently down to floor level, is no more. Even smokers can see, clearly now, that the smoking ban – the Marlborough without Marlboros – is a good thing, for regulars and staff alike.

The food these days can be surprisingly good. It was

not always so: the choice was ploughman's or chicken in a basket, or peanuts, crisps and pork scratchings. (I've never worked out exactly which part of a pig provides those extraordinary twists and twirls of trotter-hard crackling that's murder on fillings and weirdly soft centres.) Fine food, excellent, although keep a wary eye out for those 'drizzles of jus'.

The day in 1988 when the licensing laws loosened up was celebrated by everyone who'd ever arrived at the local gasping for a late lunchtime drink only to find the bell had long rung for last orders. To sit and mellow out all afternoon on that first day was a real treat, although this simply gave the resident pub bore even more hours to pontificate over his personal tankard of Old Speckled Hen.

By the way, never in all my years of pub-going have I ever heard anyone ask for a pint of Strongbow and seen those three arrows thud into the woodwork. And I have never yet worked up enough courage to stroll into the pub on the corner, order a Babycham and hope against hope that as silence descends over the entire place I am rescued by a gravel-voiced Isaac Hayes lookalike. I could have done with that bloke one day in the early '80s when an old friend I hadn't seen for a while pitched up at our house, reinvented as a New Romantic in black leather trousers, stud belt and bum-fluff moustache. We went down the local for a drink. I said, 'Do you fancy a pint?' and he ordered . . . a snowball! And did one bastard at the bar swivel round on their stool and chime in with 'Hey, *I'll* have a snowball'? You've guessed it.

Highbury or the Emirates
Football

26 May 1989 Michael Thomas nicks the League title from under Liverpool's nose at Anfield with an unforgettable stoppage-time goal, which gives the Gunners their first title for eighteen years.

I'm a long-term Arsenal fan. In geographical terms, Highbury was the nearest First Division ground to where I was born and grew up. So I could support Wealdstone, my truly local club, *and* the Arsenal without any crisis of conscience. One of the highlights of my young life was when, aged fourteen, I got a chant going at Wealdstone. It may have lacked any wit, humour, Anglo-Saxon fricatives, mention of bodily functions or vicious attacks on visiting teams, being just a pleasingly simple 'The Wealdstone (clap, clap, clap)'. But imagine my deep pleasure when I started up this clarion call all on my own and the whole of the stand joined in.

But for the old First Division, it was Arsenal: back then, the idea of supporting a team on the other side of London, let alone halfway across the country, was laughable. London was my city. And as I was from the north of it, Arsenal was my team. I first became aware of them around 1971 and the FA Cup Final, the one where Charlie George did his impression of a collapsing giraffe. There was also a touch of glamour about the Gunners. And that tapped into what had really got me going – the 1970 World Cup in Mexico. Until then, it seemed to me, the whole of football had been in black and white – cloth caps, rattles and whippets – and the footage from our illustrious 1966 victory seemed to support that. By 1970, the World Cup was much more exotic, with the games played in fabulous stadiums like the Azteca. Glamorous stadiums, glamorous girls, glamorous guys, a new international ball that looked as light as a ping-pong ball compared to the old plum pudding. And everything was in colour. It was the difference between a rainy evening in Bridlington on *It's a Knockout* and a sultry soirée in Lausanne on *Jeux sans Frontières*. Even the commentary sounded otherworldly, as if it were being beamed direct from *Apollo 12*.

Like every other kid, I made my dad drive endlessly round the neighbourhood to drain the tank before filling up at Esso to get yet another pack of World Cup coins. Now which was the one nobody could ever find – Paul Madeley?

Somewhere around 1977 I started focusing much more on the Gunners. By then I'd given up on my own football career, though I was a nippy winger, small, fast, *à la* George Armstrong. There was a period at school when one of the teachers arranged for all of us to take ballet lessons for agility and balance, and if I'd been quicker about it, I could have written a stage show. *Philly Elliott – The Musical*.

Christmas or Winterval

O, come all ye faithful

26 December 1989 The plot line for this year's *EastEnders* Christmas edition revolves around Cindy Beale giving birth on Boxing Day – only she and Simon Wicks know that the baby is his and not Ian Beale's . . .

I may have spotted a gap in the market for events organisers. To alleviate the burden of co-ordinating a family Christmas, we should be able to order one up on demand, preferably with a genuine nostalgia version to bring back the festival as it used to be. It would be the perfect retro celebration, weaving together so many of the essentials of good nostalgia: food, drink, TV, toys, board games and wall-to-wall carpeting.

Above all, it would revitalise the crêpe paper industry, which has surely been going through a slump. The decorations that we used to spend hours putting up round the living room were all made of coloured crêpe paper – the chains of paper links, card shapes that opened out to create 3D bells. It reminds me of a Kenny Everett joke, in his persona as Sid Snot, the ageing Teddy boy. 'Some people', he sniffed, 'say the soles on my shoes are crêpe. I fink they're all right myself.'

This nostalgia event would kick off first thing on

Christmas morning with the unpacking of the stocking, left at the end of the bed to be discovered on waking, and then its toes and heel explored to guess what might be inside: answer, naturally, a tangerine and a Rubik's cube (or whatever toy of the moment could be squeezed in).

There would have to be a period of discussion over exactly when the main presents could be opened, with the options ranging from 'Now, now, now!' to 'Not until we've had lunch and tidied everything away.'

The event organisers could also supply a suitable range of relatives if none were available, who could turn up just before lunch: spinster aunts a speciality, to be tucked in a corner with a small glass of sherry ('Another glass? Oh, I shouldn't, but as you insist . . .'), grandparents as ever equipped with a bottle of Blue Nun, and for a small extra fee a neighbour sporting a foulard to pop in and amuse the family with some off-colour jokes, while everyone plucks the Eat-Me dates from their plastic twigs.

Lunch would not be allowed to deviate one jot from its set pattern and the specific trimmings: the bread and cranberry sauce, roast potatoes and Brussels, the obligatory panic about the timing of the turkey in the oven, through to the brandy butter for the flamed pud (that spinster aunt will always volunteer to help polish off the brandy butter if there's some left over), and then on to the After Eight mints. Bliss.

For teenagers the lunch always fell awkwardly at the same time as the *Top of the Pops* Christmas special, the round-up of the year's Number Ones. Pre-video there had to be long and tricky negotiations with parents if you wanted to watch Slade (again) or Wizzard (again) or see Mud's Les Gray singing 'Lonely This Christmas' to a ventriloquist dummy dressed as Les, while the group's guitarist (Rob Davis – now a hugely successful songwriter, especially for Kylie) stood there with Christmas tree baubles dangling from his ears.

All feasting had to finish in time for the Queen's Speech (grannies should stand for the National Anthem) and then the party would be allowed to scatter to play with the Buckaroo or the Spirograph that had just been opened, or to try to make it all the way through a game of Monopoly without one disgruntled player overturning the board when they landed on their brother's Park Lane with two hotels *yet* again.

The reassembled party would convene for a solid evening's TV viewing, a *Generation Game*, a *Morecambe and Wise* or a *Two Ronnies* special, and then the big Christmas movie.

Around this basic pattern the retro Christmas could be tweaked to create a bespoke version. For an updated edition – the *EastEnders* Christmas package – the organisers would be happy to engineer a marriage break-up or murder between courses, or to overdo the flambéeing of the pudding and torch the house.

Now that, my friends, is a Christmas. The very familiarity of the routine provided its own comfort and joy. Of course, the planning never started until well into December. Even as kids we didn't start thinking about the possibility of presents until Bonfire Night was well out of the way, and there were no decorations on sale in September either.

Worse than the bloated, almost year-round celebrations that claim to pass for a twenty-first-century Christmas, one of the saddest developments of the past thirty-odd years has been the decline of Bonfire Night. Whereas Christmas was *en famille* – and *à table!* – Guy Fawkes Night brought the whole community together in the pitch black, with one neighbour opening up their garden and supplying the bonfire and the guy, others bringing the piping-hot sausages and jacket potatoes, maybe some toffee apples, brave dads nailing lethal Catherine wheels on to fence posts, or burying mortar-sized rockets in milk bottles deep in the flower beds. Sparklers for the kids, mulled wine for the adults. And as the last Roman candle fizzled, and the remaining sausages disappeared, a lingering, exquisite whiff of gunpowder trailed across the azaleas. Try to organise something similar next November – no can do, Health and Safety, sorry, pal. Homemade fun – no, I'm afraid that's been cancelled. The sausages are fine, but you must apply for an exterior catering licence and we may get back to you by March.

There are a few tattered remains of the traditional Christmas to hang on to, so long as the local council hasn't run out of money for the street decorations and your turkey's not been liberated by Hugh Fearnley-Whittingstall. At least leave us the name. I'm delighted that my kids can learn about the Chinese New Year, make lanterns for Diwali and understand the meaning of Eid and Yom Kippur. But, please, don't call Christmas Winterval. That's plain wrong.

———

Christmas or Winterval

It's perverse. If any carol (a.k.a. Winterval anthem) singers come round and wish me 'Happy Winterval', I can guarantee they will receive a cracker shoved so high up their parson's nose that they'll be hitting the highest notes in 'Ding, Dong, Merrily on High' with the greatest of ease. No problems. Merry bleedin' Christmas.

Retro-spection

If this book were a '70s TV special, at this point Mike Yarwood would put away Harold Wilson's pipe, adjust his cuffs, announce 'and now this is me', and promptly massacre some great show tune. Or Janet Webb would brush aside Eric and Ernie in the middle of 'Bring Me Sunshine' and thank us all for watching 'me and my little show'. And Larry Grayson would turn to camera at the end of *The Generation Game*, top lip quivering, telling us – 'I love you all very much'. I'm still working on my own theme song, so meanwhile I hope you've had fun on this journey back in time, a round trip to a long-lost world of coq au vin and Cortinas, *Crackerjack* and the Carpenters. And make sure you savour those memories while you can. Because there'll come a day when a jaunt down Memory Lane turns into a wander down Amnesia Avenue . . .

Acknowledgements

First of all I'd like to thank my mum and dad for having me, and for ensuring I was born in the '60s so that I could write a book about the '70s and '80s. Nicely planned. Thanks also to my brother Robert, and to Celia, Tom and Emily.

Huge thanks to my agent Gilly Sanguinetti for her guidance and support over the years and on this project in particular. Thanks also to Gordon Wise at Curtis Brown and my editor Antonia Hodgson for bringing the book together, and to Kirsteen Astor, Philip Parr, Vivien Redman, Jenny Richards, Emma Williams and the whole Little, Brown team for their help and expertise.

To Matthew Graham, Ashley Pharoah, Tony Jordan and all at Team Kudos for the gift of the Gene Genie.

To Paul Paterson – forty-five years of friendship still going strong – and to Gareth Hughes and Paul Mendelson, just cos I like you.

Thanks to Bob Cherry at the Cropredy Bridge Garage, Simon Cook, Marie de Freitas, Martin Elliott, Scott Harrison and the staff of the Campanile, Marmande.

Special thanks to Mr Dodd for turning my rants and ramblings into some kind of prose, just for me to turn them back into a rant, with added swearing.

And finally to my good friend, Thin Lizzy's Scott Gorham, who contributed absolutely nothing to this book due to the fact that he can't remember most of the '70s.
